ON THE OTHER SIDE OF THE FENCE

Sharron Murgatroyd

Romney Publications

Published by
Romney Publications
351 Exning Road, Newmarket, Suffolk CB8 0AU.

First edition October 2001

ISBN 0-9528566-9-7 Paperback
ISBN 0-9541587-0-9 Hardback

Designed and Typeset by
Equine Veterinary Journal Ltd, Newmarket, Suffolk, UK.

Printed by
Geerings of Ashford Ltd, Kent, UK.

Front Cover
Photograph of Sharron riding *Songbird Miracle* (1991) by 'P.H. Photography'
Photograph of Sharron (2001) by 'The Photographers', Fordham, Suffolk, UK.
Cover design by Equine Veterinary Jounal Ltd, Newmarket, Suffolk, UK.

Back Cover
Photograph by Neville Howes, 'The Photographers', Fordham, Suffolk, UK.

Other titles by Sharron Murgatroyd
Jump Jockeys Don't Cry
Nil Desperandum
Pony Days

CONTENTS

Dedication

Alan & Jan Bailey
Who made my dream a reality
And supported me throughout my career
Thank you
For the magic and the mayhem!

All the owners and trainers I rode for
Especially David & the late Alison Thom.

My friends
On both sides of the fence!
Who have filled my life with a richness
That money cannot buy
You know who you are.

My Mother & Family
The journey is not over yet!

Foreword

I remember first meeting Sharron in the ladies' changing room before an amateur flat race in which we were both riding. I was the young, probably spoilt, no doubt self-important rich kid riding horses trained by my father. Sharron was the hard-working, smiling tough nut wearing a lucky jumper knitted by her mum that had MURGY on the front of it. She would have kicked me into shape in two seconds if she had felt the need but to her eternal credit, she was warm, friendly and funny. I felt awkward until I got to know the other girls, feeling all along that I could easily be ostracised because of my privileged position, but Sharron and a few others ensured that I was not.

They took the mick mercilessly out of my accent, told me that my hands were too soft to ever have done a proper day's work, laughed at me when I tried to be too clever, sympathised with my weight problems and slapped me on the back if I won. In other words, they treated me like a mate and I loved it. I joined in with the banter, gave as good as I got and adored riding in races as much for the comradeship as the thrill of competition.

The most memorable day in my very short riding career was made even more so by Sharron herself. I was involved in a very tight contest all year with Sharron's good friend Lydia Pearce for the title of champion lady rider. We got to the final race of the season at Chepstow with Lydia just ahead of me on points. I needed to win the race to overtake her and claim the title that I had just missed out on the year before. I was riding a horse called 'Respectable Jones', trained by my uncle Toby Balding, while Lydia was on a decent horse trained by R. Bostock. Neither of us were favourite, but both knew we could and, in my case, had to win. Sharron, as was more usual than her talent deserved, was on a long shot.

I made all of the running and never saw another horse until I was nearing the winning post and looked behind to see Lydia pushing for all she was worth in second. 'Respectable Jones' hung on in front, I punched the air (nearly falling off in the effort) and Lydia, sportingly, cantered up to congratulate me. The other girls were very kind but one in particular had realised the significance of the day before we got to the races and had taken the trouble to bring along a bottle of champagne to award to whichever one of myself or Lydia won the championship.

That person was Sharron and despite the fact that Lydia was her friend, she was as pleased for me as anyone and sprayed me with bubbles as I walked back into the changing room. I have never forgotten that gesture and felt more like 'one of the girls' on that day than ever.

There is a poem included in this book called One River, in which Sharron writes:

In my corner of time
Where for me the living is fine
With light and dark
Day and night and half night.
Following a path with many places to go
Destined to live my life - taking on every fight.

All these things I know
And I can see my river that flows.
If only you could see me
Like you did before
Then one river could flow.

I see Sharron as she was before, I see her standing there in her breeches and boots with her funny knitted MURGY jumper and her smile, always the life and soul of the weighing room, always the first with a joke and the last one to leave. When I look at her now, I see her in exactly the same way, only sitting rather than standing.

I admired her before and I admire her now because she knows what she wants out of life and has continued to work hard to get it. Reading this book will make you understand the daily difficulties she faces, whether they be overcoming pain, dealing with tricky hotels or ignorant racegoers and to share with her the fun she has in life - jumping out of aeroplanes, riding, dancing, scuba diving and laughing.

This book will make you realise what it is that makes her special and it is not her disability. The fall at Bangor did not destroy the Sharron Murgatroyd we always knew, it merely accentuated the strong elements in her character that already existed. She was always special. One of the positive outcomes of her paralysis is that more people can share her strength and benefit from it because of her writing and because of this book in particular. For that, we should all be grateful.

I wish her all the success in the world and hope that she continues to push back the barriers placed in her way, for her own sake and for that of others, so that by the time they reach the same point in the race, the hurdle may already have been knocked out of the way for them.

Clare Balding

Introduction

In this book I will be addressing many subjects. I will tell you things that may make you feel uncomfortable. I will take you to the depths of despair - maybe even to euphoric heights! I want to make you ache with laughter - cry at the situation of how insignificant some people can make you feel with a tactless remark on a sensitive day.

I want this book to give you an insight into both my world of disability and of the people who choose to be 'Carers'. The coming together of many different personalities who find they are spending days and nights with people they have nothing in common with. Well, that is not really correct, there is something in common - my needs...

If this is not what you want to read about, then I suggest you put the book back on the shelf.

A decade has passed and many things have changed in my life. Ten years of re-establishing my identity, of pushing boundaries to the limit and evaluating my future. I will tell you throughout the book how lucky and fortunate I feel - and how I would not swap my life with anybody else's. This is my truth...

I want you to know truth and fact... TRUTH: Two out of three people think everybody in a wheelchair is below average intelligence! FACT: 15 people in the UK will break their back or neck this week, leaving them paralysed for life.

Having read this book you may wake up one morning and think 'but it won't happen to me' - I did and it did. When you turn over the page you will be with me:

On the Other Side of the Fence

Attitude

Keep your face to the sun
And
You cannot see the shadows

Determination

The race is not always
To the swift
But to those who keep on running

Courage

You cannot discover new oceans
Until you have courage
To lose sight of the shore

Success

Success is a journey
Not a destination

Not my words - but good words...

Longing

Come to me in my dreams
And then by day I shall be well again.
For then the night will more than pay
The hopeless longing of the day.

Comest as thou camest a thousand times
A messenger from radiant climes.
And smile on thy new world
And be as kind to others as to me,
Or as they never came in sooth
Come now and let me dream a truth
And part my hair and kiss my brow
And say my love why sufferest thou.

Come to me in my dreams
And then by day I shall be well again.
For then the night will more than pay
The hopeless longing of the day.

By
Matthew Arnold

CHAPTER ONE

HAVE WHEELS WILL TRAVEL

On Thursday 3rd October 1996 my house was like Piccadilly Circus - it was the day of the launch of my first published book, *Jump Jockeys Don't Cry*. It had taken me three long years but at last it had come to fruition. Despite failing my 11-plus, feeling I'd failed in my chosen career by letting down people who had supported me (paying a high price for one bad decision) - I had now achieved something tangible for both myself and the doubters, that couldn't be overlooked. Even so, the blue shiny cover bearing my face and name still seemed as though it had been done by an impostor.

I really wanted to train horses but soon realised that this was not one of my better ideas. I felt inadequate to do that job with my degree of disability. The entirety of my life had been wrenched out of my hands - leaving a gaping hole. So when some friends originally suggested I write a book about my life and the severity of my accident, I thought that maybe this could just help fill the void and I would remain as near to my able-bodied life as possible.

I suppose they reckoned on my story being relayed through somebody who was actually 'a writer' but there was only one way and that was in my own words. "I'm writing a book", I told people who asked what I was doing and it sounded good - I wasn't just sitting about all day doing nothing. I used to like writing essays when I had attended school and I'd written poetry from my years as a teenager. It started as a façade but once the first few pages materialised, the more feasible it became. My saving grace was being able to string a few words together and - with a little help - them making sense!

The hubbub that surrounded me was manic, telephone ringing constantly, people arriving from different parts of the country - it was going to be an unbelievable night. A cross-section of family, childhood and school friends and those I'd made since entering racing, right through to top racing personalities such as Lester Piggott and John Francome would be sharing an evening together to celebrate my first literary endeavour. Although I was well aware it could never be a best seller and I hadn't felt the sort of euphoria that came with riding a winner - it had nonetheless given me back some self-esteem, some sense of purpose and a new direction to my life.

In the evening at the Bedford Lodge Hotel I found myself the centre of attention and felt daunted; all this just didn't seem right! Under different circumstances, if I'd been able-bodied, this would not have fazed me but my changed image posed its own problems. The kindness of all the well-meaning people involved in helping me to produce this work and the many guests made me feel unworthy. I felt self-conscious about my appearance even though Michelle Kelly, my helper, had gone to great pains with my hair, make-up and clothes (a new beaded trouser suit) which had drawn favourable comments earlier when I blew the whistle at Newmarket Town's ground for the start of a football match.

Looking back, it was an overwhelming night for many - not least my mother, Thelma, whose mixed feelings of pride and sadness could never be measured. Also my former employers were there - Alan Bailey and David Thom (DT) - who had not only encouraged me but also backed this up with the opportunity to race-ride regularly. So it proved to be a night of high emotion for all. The atmosphere was almost palpable as relatives and friends from afar circulated comfortably within this different environment which I had sought for myself. Some used this occasion to have their books autographed by the well-known people who were there. Of course I didn't mind even when sometimes I was the last to sign! It was a night of celebration and it panned out easily until 3am.

Although I had made a few appearances on television prior to my accident and several since, this would be the first time I would deliver a speech in front of so many people. Surprisingly, it came quite easily and as all those gathered knew my wicked sense of humour, I didn't feel inhibited. I wish I could have been in as much demand when I was race-riding as I was on that night - everybody wanted to congratulate me - including numerous Press requests. Miss Popular, or what?

Peter Rossdale, who set up Romney Publications to publish my work, had a great team behind him and Lisa Brundell arranged and handled promotion of the book. She was both enthusiastic and confident which made me more than happy to meet each engagement. It turned out to be a hectic schedule but well worth it.

The two people who had collaborated with Peter Rossdale in putting *Jump Jockeys* on the bookshelf, were a long-standing and dear friend of Peter's - Ian Wallace; and semi-retired publisher - Ian McIntyre, who was also a friend. Ian Wallace (who I had never heard of), the well known singer and performer on 'My Music' and also of the Hippopotamus song, gave me great encouragement and guidance - and Ian McIntyre did the same but with a much more business-like approach. His input with my next book would be invaluable.

Both men had faced adversity in different ways. Ian Wallace had been struck down with tuberculosis of the spine at the age of 24. He had spent two years in hospital, but still managed to write a musical comedy play amongst other things!

Ian McIntyre had lost his first wife and later re-married a lady who already had wheelchair-bound twin boys with muscular dystrophy.

The first time I met him I knew the book would be safe from ridicule, as he was a professional man who knew the business. He smacked of power and knowledge, which wasn't daunting for me (I'd worked with men who were the same or thought they were); I was pleased. I felt I was back - back in business - albeit a very different one. These were men of substance and integrity.

By mid December after the launch, I had been on Channel 4's racing programme, The Morning Line; Declan Murphy had interviewed me for the Racing Channel (having had a life-threatening race fall that eventually ended his riding career); been featured on Radio Cambridge (presented by Christopher South); had travelled to London by 10am for a live interview on Woman's Hour and on the same day had been a guest on Five Live with Sybil Rusco. I was meeting so many different people interested in lady jockeys, but one of my most memorable interviews would have to be the one with the ex-rugby international - Cliff Morgan - who came to my home and on the following Saturday delivered a superb show. Made me sound good! Thank you, Cliff!

One of my major undertakings on 4th December was to fly to Dublin and then travel to Dungannon in Northern Ireland where I had been invited to make a speech at a function attended by over 150 guests, both able-bodied and handicapped. It was Disability Awareness Day, the message being 'Life Does Not Stop'. Whilst I was in Ireland I also did two other radio shows and then travelled back down to Dublin to appear on a morning TV programme (like Richard and Judy - who previously declined my appearance and promotion of the book on their show!).

I quite took to this promotional work but obviously without my two lady helpers, Janet Boston and Michelle Kelly, who washed, dressed and made me presentable, none of this could have happened. With Lisa proving a very able driver and organiser our trip was one to remember - even though unfortunately Janet slipped on the ice and broke her arm the night of the function. This prevented her from accompanying me to 10 Downing Street where I had been invited to meet the Prime Minister. Martin Raymond (jockey's agent) had kindly offered to pick us up at Stansted where we had flown in from Dublin and drove us directly to Whitehall. We had been told about security procedures, so after some last-minute hitches that involved Janet's name being transferred into that of Michelle's (very dodgy indeed), we were allowed in!

It was a wonderful evening and this time I was pleased the stair lift that is installed at Number 10 for their wheelchair visitors was 'OUT OF ORDER'! Mrs Major apologised and asked an equerry to take us to the function room by way of another lift. As everybody else took the direct route to be introduced to the host, Michelle and I went via two other rooms. The equerry put us at ease straight away by giving us the run down of the evening. Everybody wore a name badge and was encouraged to speak to whoever they wanted. He pointed out some interesting items in the rooms that only we were privy to and, mounted in a glass case with a shiny varnished wood stand, was a white round ball. "Oh that's the moon rock that Neil Armstrong brought back," he told us casually. "Wow, moon rock," I exclaimed - it doesn't take a lot to impress me!

We met many personalities; I was thrilled to be introduced to Dick Francis (former jockey turned successful novelist) by his son Felix and we discussed racing and writing. I also had a few words with actor Derek Fowlds, arty nun Sister Wendy and Des Lynham who everyone knows. The two equerries kept making sure we were all right and topped us up with the best red wine I've ever tasted. Definitely 'agreeable claret' as my old riding buddy Elaine Bronson would say.

Unfortunately Mr Major had been unavoidably detained so only caught the last half-hour of the evening. I had met the PM once before at Huntingdon Races on Boxing Day 1990, where I had two rides. The recently retired Clerk of the Course Hugo Bevan introduced me as 'one of our many good lady jump riders', but I didn't think for one moment that Mr Major would remember so I never recalled the occasion. There was one story I couldn't resist telling him though, and this was about his daughter Elizabeth. She had met the (sadly now late) Alison Thom and asked if she could ride out as she hoped to have a ride in a National Hunt Flat Race, which is basically a race for potential jumpers without jumps. Ali asked DT if Elizabeth Major could ride out and he'd said yes - without looking up from reading the 'Timeform' racing book.

A few days later the then Miss Major duly turned up to ride out first lot. As they were walking around waiting for their instructions DT said 'morning' to his new pilot. First lot went well and, making polite conversation, DT asked Miss Major what her father did.

"He's John Major," she replied. DT, on not getting the answer he asked for, raised his voice:

"I asked you what he did - not what his bloody name was!"

We arrived home late and tired but, after a day's rest, I had my first signing at Newmarket's local bookshop, Tindalls. They had dressed the front window wonderfully, displaying my book with eye-catching effect. It went quite well even though I had arranged for Rent-A-Mob to attend (these included some of the girls that worked for me with their families and a few friends) to avoid the embarrassment of sitting in an empty shop! Book sales were going very well and all my friends knew what they could buy for Christmas presents!

I often wondered what would happen when all the commotion died down; would I be feeling lonely and left out? This question had arisen when I spent a couple of weeks in a disabled unit, which is often referred to as a halfway house, before returning home to 'Becklyn', my bungalow in Kennett, from Oswestry Orthopaedic Hospital. The commotion had not died down then and it didn't wane for the next few years, as I later came to realise.

Jump Jockeys Don't Cry was favourably received in racing circles although a number of the boys said they would wait until they retired before they read it and apparently some of them do cry - I never knew that!

As before when I was hospitalised, cards and letters flooded in, but this time they were of appreciation. To my amazement, people from all walks of life had found solace by reading my book. I was overwhelmed by the impact of what I felt was a meagre offering, as it seemed to touch so many people. Five years had passed since my accident - whatever dreams or aspirations I had before were borne out in fantasy - five years, gone in a blink as I survived within this surreal world.

Saying I felt I'd been lucky was often mentioned throughout, and with the encouragement from family and the racing fraternity (which know no bounds) failure to cope was non-negotiable. I had been a wilful little girl and my mother had brought me up to be a strong, independent woman. The need to put something back was always going to be there. I wasn't comfortable just to sit and do nothing and as the physical pain had abated a little by now as Mr El Masry (the Oswestry spinal unit's consultant) said it would, I wanted and needed to be doing something. I needed to try and help in some capacity by showing others that there can still be fulfilment in life even after such a powerful body blow. Of course it may not be the aspiration they had hoped for, as mine was to be champion lady jockey. It would just be different.

Anyway, how many people get what they hope and work for and love? Maybe I felt I had to prove that this brave persona I had taken on wasn't only an act? I knew there were still some demons lurking at the back of beyond, but that was my own private warfare. I would deal with them in my own time, but this was the beginning of another phase of my life and I realised that the publication of *Jump Jockeys* had provided me with the perfect vehicle.

It would be a lie to say I didn't bask in the compliments I received for my first literary work, probably because most people wondered how a former racehorse stable girl was capable of putting finger to keyboard, with no ghost writer or higher education.

The New Year proved to be as hectic as the end of the last following the publication of *Jump Jockeys*. I tried to savour the moments that followed - but the aftermath wasn't all good. Up until now I had, in a way, been in a cocoon, surrounded by people who had known me before or had come to know me through my predicament. Subsequently I was treated as a fairly normal person with at least half a brain! I had spent two years organising my new life - just getting on with it - and three years writing a book with eyes wide open, or so I thought. I'd taken in the numerous pleasures of life that had previously passed me by, when I was only interested in where and when my horses were running and whether I'd 'get the ride or get the jock'!

As spring arrived there were still requests via my publishers for me to sign particular names of purchasers of *Jump Jockeys*. We had a scheme whereby I signed 'Best Wishes, Sharron' on every book personally and on a good day I could sign up to 20 books in an hour. I signed the books with a felt tip pen secured in a strap and tied to my left hand. I was right handed but the left had no choice and soon became accustomed to its new role. Two days were never the same even using identical equipment, so there were times when the pen would be at a good angle and whilst it was in a good position, I made full use of it. One particular day when it was flowing my mother suggested that I attempt a further 10, and as she was one of my biggest promoters, I enthusiastically agreed. That session saw me achieve a personal best of 40 copies - competitive streak still there! This obviously made signing sessions easier because I then only had to put 'To Whoever… '.

Just as I thought things were calming down, the Injured Jockeys' Fund asked me if I could go to the Cheltenham Festival and do a book signing on the stand. Would I go to Cheltenham? Try and stop me! This also fitted in well as the versatile Richard Phillips - who had become a friend through racing and has proved to be a very able racehorse trainer - was presenting live interviews and the latest racing news from the Cheltenham Festival track on local radio. He was obviously running out of people to interview and asked me if I would like to do it. An unequivocal 'yes' was the answer. We would chat, plug the book and I would read a poem I had written about Cheltenham. My timeslot was after one of the most respected ladies-of-the-turf, the formidable Mrs Dickinson. Richard, knowing that I had previously worked for the Dickinsons, interacted our interviews which worked well. I was meeting every engagement I could and still enjoying it!

At this stage I didn't know if I would ever write another book but found, by the end, I'd actually enjoyed writing *Jump Jockeys*. I had started writing a short story a couple of months before my fall. If it had ever been finished (which I doubt because I was too busy with my racing life), like my poetry it would have probably remained unseen except by my closest of confidants.

I had been programmed in Oswestry's orthopaedic hospital to focus positively on every aspect I was capable of doing, even though the only thing my whole being knew at that time was racing. My love for racehorses would never die but my involvement with them would soon start to take a secondary place. I concentrated on the things I could do and strove to do well - regrettably leaving aside an enormous part of my life that was no longer pertinent. I realised I had a brain - it just needed a lot of exercise - like before, 110% effort required or nothing.

Racing Away

Thundering hooves racing past
On an afternoon that brings the feeling back.
That feeling that makes the living fine
In wind, or rain, or bright sunshine.
Thundering crowds shouting loud
As they provide the electric sound.
We watch our beloved horses race
To win is a bonus, just come home safe.

Thundering ground sometimes you fall
But the glory of winning with a vengeance calls.
Then who knows the twist of fate
You won today and the feeling's great.
Thundering hooves racing away
Adrenaline pounds each and every day.
Sheer precision when riding so fast
A thank-you please for a valiant cast.

Thundering silence when all has gone
But the memories urge you all to keep strong.
Even when the darkest clouds
Menacingly gather closing you down.
Thundering hooves can you hear them call?
So sorry it was you taking that fall,
You rode the race, took centre stage
Look towards the sun don't let your light fade.

CHAPTER TWO

FRIDAY'S CHILD

I was born at 4am on Friday 5th February 1960 - I was awake at 4am on Friday 2nd August 1991 and, after the 5.20pm race that day, I was no longer a woman of purpose; I had been rendered childlike.

With the passing of time, I have established a foundation where I live comfortably - I am one of the lucky ones.

If that Friday had never come, then neither would these very special women who now share my life. They soon came to understand my wicked and sarcastic sense of humour (I broke them in gently) and how I could exaggerate the smallest of happenings into an epic story! This was not ever going to be a mundane job, as I took it upon myself to spice things up a bit. I think they will tell you how I have retained my enthusiasm for life - but it still hasn't been an altogether smooth ride for any of us. Some of them have had their own adversity to face and I would like to think that I have been able to help them through their difficult times.

We have all grown over the last few years, even Janet Boston and Joan Chapman (the latter now a relief worker) who are the oldest of my ladies - next in age come Nancy Chambers and Shirley Marshall (who took over from Joan), myself and Carey Cooper, and last but not least Michelle Kelly. Gabrielle Dick (the physio from hell!) must be included in my band of ladies as she has been treating me since the time I spent in a halfway house. I'm sure it must seem longer to her than it does for me, or should that be the other way round - I'll think about that one! Helen Offord, my beautician (that phrase 'my whatever' always sounds as if they are exclusive to you - well, I think so anyway!), has also known me from the first week I returned home, eyebrows and fingernails are all down to her - oh, and the waxing. It only took me four years of asking, "Are you sure that wax isn't too hot?" and her replying, "Yes," before I realised she knew what she was doing! I was lucky not to get my head waxed! Every other Monday morning we either listen to our latest music fad or put the world to rights; acting raucous and naughty or sometimes we are comfortable with silence. Agency worker Julie Prime comes in on a weekend and Petra Van Doorn, who had spent so much time with me in the early years, has gone back to Sweden after her marriage breakdown.

I was fortunate that Janet (later to be nicknamed the Water Drinker by Joan, as she does not partake in a glass of the agreeable claret or anything else alcoholic!) was available from the beginning to do a few sleep-ins. This led to her having a career change, so now instead of looking after horses she looks after me. It has worked out well even though I must admit I felt uncomfortable at times. Janet is the only one who knew me before my debilitating accident and I suppose I felt more stripped of my dignity with her because of this.

We (Ali Thom, Penny who worked with us, and myself) had always behaved ourselves around Janet, when working for David Thom, no swearing or silliness in front of her and we had been brought up in the age when you respected your elders. Now she was working for me, I had to ask her to do various jobs. Joan used to be a nurse and all the other girls had been involved in this line of work but they hadn't known me - they didn't know me - they didn't know 'the me' that Janet did…

I have control, but I don't have full control of my life. I traded that in when I took my chance at Bangor. My dependency on 24 hour care has its restrictions but to say I've been lucky to have a long-standing and loyal team of girls and ladies with me, to make sure I live my life, as near to how I damn well like, is an understatement. I could never do their job. The balance isn't too hard to keep and although we have raucous times I still yearn for my privacy. We all need our own space.

My obsessive behaviour is a worry! Sometimes when I'm in one of my brief states of frustrating paranoia, I feel like I'm under a microscope being monitored, with the heading - 'Behaviour of a wheelchair-bound forty-something spinster.' The re-emergence of David Bowie on the English music scene in '99 was a good example of this. My vinyl collection of songs that so encapsulated me in my teenage years was re-born. I built up another mass collection of the 'God of music' on CDs. I spent endless nights videoing interviews and concerts, carefully cutting out the adverts. I taped Wembley, Glastonbury and numerous VH1 programmes. So it's Bowie full blast, he sings all the right songs to me, releasing any tension (I know most of you could just kick the cat, but I haven't got a cat!). I then become tranquil, the monitored microscope phobia goes out of the window - and I'm sure his wife Iman wouldn't mind. I have always loved his music.

There is no denying that there can be fraught times whilst working in such close proximity, and on a deeply personal level. In fact, at times we bug each other! I can't stand atmosphere and if any of the girls are unhappy or upset - by me or anyone else - I want it sorted out, in the open so we can deal with it and move on. Those times are few and far between but there were incidents in the early days when there was friction between the girls, and on occasions this included my mother. I had to be the arbitrator as I could see both sides of the issue. Obviously there were conflicting ideas of what was best for me.

That being said, I have not had a big turnover of staff as often seems to be the case, so I can't be all that bad! Fact.

I have tried to keep my home as it was meant to be. My door is always open and I have a constant stream of visitors or friends, some staying overnight - my bungalow has earned the nickname 'Hotel Becklyn' and is also used as a drop-in place to shower and change for any Lambourn travellers (you know who you are).

Admission's free - you pay to get out! I love these times and if my mum isn't here making them welcome with delicious cakes and other culinary delights then whoever is here is very obliging with whatever is in my fridge or cupboards. We don't stand on ceremony though, so there are times when they have to help themselves! It gives me particular pleasure when the roles are reversed and one of the girls has a cuppa made for them.

I often wonder how others feel in my predicament. Do they get the five star treatment that resident and customers at The Hotel Becklyn do - or are they made to feel like 'the next task on a list of paper'?

These are the ten rules and regulations at Becklyn:

1. First and foremost, we must have as much fun as possible.
2. Life is for living.
3. My ablutions are a taboo subject and we use euphemisms for everything between my neck and knees!
4. Honesty and loyalty is both given and received.
5. Grievances must be aired, with swearing if necessary.
6. Nobody is referred to as a 'Carer'.
7. I am not immune to humorous terminology regarding my wheelchair-bound status.
8. Fashion trends must be followed to their own specification.
9. We operate a system of swings and roundabouts - flexible working hours/changes in shifts/kids/dogs/etc.
10. They must be the crème-de-la-crème and take no crème-de-la-crap from me; well, not often!

The restrictions of a nursing regime went out of the window after about a year never to be seen or heard of again! I attribute my wellbeing to the whole team; well, yes it is true, I am team leader, so no abrasions, bruises or marks go unnoticed and we pride ourselves on that. Although some may think that I make light of what is a serious subject, I know only too well how 20 minutes of sitting on an unsuitable surface can alter the whole course of day-to-day life for months. This can run into years even when every necessary precaution is taken.

There seems to be a fallacy about paralysis not causing physical pain but in reality there are many types of discomfort. People say, "I thought you couldn't feel your legs". I cannot feel them to touch but I still endure root pain. This is pain at the root of the spinal nerves and affects my whole body - some days are worse than others - so it's not all that grim.

Fact: Root pain is one of the most debilitating side effects for paraplegics and tetraplegics.

The muscles in my neck and shoulders are often taut and knotted, which is caused by their lack of full range movement and spasticity. It is ironic that my lack of mobility causes pain, and often physiotherapy - which ranges from passive leg movement, arm-strengthening exercises and standing upright in a frame to having deep connective muscle tissue massage, which relieves tension around my neck and shoulders by bringing oxygen and blood into the muscles - also causes a degree of pain. This is never going to lessen but the body does become accustomed to it.

There are a number of pain-relieving drugs for root pain and spasticity but one is always advised to cope without them as dependency can cause addiction, the end result being a higher and higher dosage. A small amount of alcohol can help - for example one pint of beer - "How much?!" "One pint of beer is helpful in relieving pain and spasm." "How many glasses of red wine is that?" Unfortunately, drink, even for medicinal purposes, is only available here after 6pm - sadly - except at Christmas and Bank Holidays when my family is staying with me. I have found that mental and psychological factors play a part in pain severity and keeping the mind active and occupied can help alleviate pain. So if you're mental and a bit of a pyscho - you're probably pissed now!

My ladies understand all of this and know that it goes with the territory. For my part, as Anthony Hopkins said in the film 'Shadowlands', "The pain now is part of the happiness then, and that's the deal".

There was this enormous power in me which I took every opportunity to impress on newcomers - that I had been doing a job, I had been living, walking and breathing just like them. I felt that I was almost reneging on other disabled people as I strove to keep my past alive and continually ignored my physical state. An outsider who does not know me said, "because I was relatively newly injured I was still in denial".

This comment seemed very strange to me as it had been seven years since I acquired my wheels. So what was wrong with living as normally as possible - and why was it such a big deal to others that I hang a notice around my neck with the word 'Disabled' on it?

As long as the girls and I are comfortable with our set-up - is it for anybody else to judge how I go about my daily life? Surely the whole point of this matter is that people live, whether disabled or not, the way they see fit. More broadly, I understand the underlying issues that face us all in a society which isn't necessarily wheelchair friendly but I see changes being made, albeit slowly, within the environment and I personally have no axe to grind. Unfortunately, out in the big world there are people whose behaviour towards wheelchair users is moving even slower than the building works, as I have found out!

So, my present state of affairs and that of my ladies is buoyant; everyone works professionally together and friendships have evolved - this in turn reflects on me. Situation perfect.

My day starts at 8am, except on weekends, when it is, "Oh, come in when you like - about 10" (well, I do need my beauty sleep). Monday, Wednesday and Friday mornings are showering days and can take up to two hours before I'm presentable; I also have physio on a Friday. If there were less chat and more work, this time could possibly be shortened a little. When Nancy (Nanceroony, Social Services input), who arrives at 6pm on the dot every night (apart from Tuesday when Anne comes in) to cook my dinner, and Shirley (Shirley-wirly, my own input) start, then even I have a job to get a word in! I also manage to shower on Saturdays and Sundays thanks to agency input and over the last couple of years Julie (Flopsy) has worked every weekend so I've been lucky to have the same person. Tuesday, Thursday and Friday have now become physio mornings and, after a quick flick with a flannel or shower, I'm ready to give it everything - most of the time. The girls work by a rota system (subject to change at any given time).

Nothing is set in stone at Becklyn and everyone plays a different part, working in and around whatever is going on in my life or theirs - sometimes it is quiet, other times it's manic. I find that they all have their individual ways of doing things but this does not pose a problem for me, an onlooker; where once I lay inhibited and degraded by attention to the more personal parts of my anatomy - now I'm mercifully indifferent.

Obviously this has not happened overnight. It has taken a long time for me to surrender my immobile limbs, let go of my inherent feelings and detach mind from body for this period of time, which should not be allowed to exist for your worst enemy. Truth.

If That Friday Had Never Come

Locked in a sleepless night - Till wakefulness gives in at dawn - And if yesterday's Friday never came - I'd be rising now instead of sleeping till you call - I wish it was still Thursday - Then pain and wake would be - Never a beleaguered trial for you - As it is for me.

***You Joan**; Dress me gently - As my body burns with fire - And today I'm unresponsive - Lost from love but not desire - Knowing if that Friday had never come - You wouldn't know me at all - And I lay nearly sleeping into sleep I need to fall.*

***You Gabrielle**; Next to appear - Unusually I'm quiet - But not yet dead you fear! With pain in my head and neck - No rolling or sitting today - Just help me to stand up - In the wooden frame - Neither would you know me if that Friday never came.*

***You Janet**; Arrive at midday - I'm beginning to feel better now - Not so dull and grey - They tell you I talk too much - Satirical in what I say - Striving to make them laugh - And drive my pain away - But you're the only one remembering me from Thursday - As if that Friday had never come.*

***You Nancy**; Right on time - To feed me food and wine - Sitting in my living room I'm glad that I'm alive - So hard for you to ever know - If that Friday had never come - I reached for diamonds in the sky - Alas they were never won.*

***You Carey**; Come and go - But always try to be - Accommodating as you can with things concerning me - Another who would never know - If that Friday never came - How much I loved my life - And liked to play the game.*

***You Michelle**; To put me in my bed - Looking bright and cheerful - Dressed in vibrant red - I like to see you all happy - Though sometimes it is said - I wasn't always laughing - And if that Friday never came - I wonder where we'd be now - No life that is the same.*

***You Petra**; First to share - My coming home to stay - Knowing when in silence - I had nothing I wanted to say - Two very different people - Who shared some poignant times - We also had some fun - And never would I know you - If that Friday hadn't come.*

Footnote: These were the ladies who were looking after me at the time.

CHAPTER THREE

THE THINGS I DIDN'T SAY

Now as I skim the pages, checking that I don't repeat the many highs and lows of those first five years, one major fault screams at me, leaps out of the pages - that is, the things I didn't say.

Too green or shy a fledgling embarking into a totally alien world of writing and publishing. Needing to be needed and yet at the same time so brave and bold. This was always going to keep me who I was, first and foremost - a lady jockey - a jump jockey; and I was determined not to be diminished. So here I am three books later with so much more to say. I can hear those of you who know me saying, "If my legs could run as fast as my mouth, I'd be sporting golden medallions"!

I'll begin with a recollection of an evening's racing. After that there are many tales to tell as I delve into my past, analyse my present, and wonder what the future will bring.

On a lovely July evening back in 1993, Alvin Stardust was doing a gig after the last race. I had gone to Newmarket races with a helper who was not altogether interested in horses. This was the first time I had ventured out to my old domain without a posse of racing friends, or media interest that had arisen from Injured Jockeys' fund-raising. There would be lots of people that I knew and maybe, in my naïvety, I thought it would be just the same as before I became a wheelchair jockey. But there was definitely a disquieting shift of reaction towards me, my wheels posing a problem for some people, and I would be pushing against those boundaries for many more years to come.

Memories of blue and white colours flashing past the winning post and rapturous applause were again to the fore in my mind, as I watched the runners from the second race being led into the winner's enclosure. The usual buzz of the racecourse was evident even though I was no longer totally involved. I was making out that it was the appearance of Alvin Stardust that enticed me along, rather than the evening's runners and riders...

Frankie Dettori wins the prize for the biggest smile of the evening after steering Big Pat to victory. I watch - their glow of satisfaction seeping into me, as connections unsaddle. A job well done. I know them - I know how they feel. They go to celebrate, turning right towards the Member's Bar, unaware that I am even there. I am asked, "Where to now?" in a bored, uninterested voice, but I do not answer…there is no answer.

The crowd begins to disperse from around the enclosure and I feel uncomfortable - frowned upon because I am in the way. The endless 'Excuse me please' becomes embarrassing, as do polite but hurried smiles from people that I know. I want to tell them I am still the same, but to them it is sad - to them it is a shame - and to avoid me is easier than to face me in a wheelchair. I understand, I tell myself, and ask, how would I react? This time two years ago my predicament was unforeseeable as I stood by the winners' enclosure exchanging pleasantries. One of the 'racing set', one of the 'lady jockeys' - "Well done yesterday", as I am patted on the back. They did not have to explain why because I was still savouring my victory.

I am pushed away from the enclosure as the applause that was once for me begins to fade from my thoughts. Back in the present I give directions to my driver. A good position to watch Alvin Stardust and his band is essential for me now, whereas yesterday it would not have been remotely important. The band strikes up…and the roars and shouts of punters and the vivid colours of dancing, prancing racehorses on a sunny evening are a far cry from the aged leather-clad rocker who appears in a cloud of simulated smoke on a makeshift stage. The expressions on faces around me change as bodies begin to sway to the music. Then by the time Alvin gets to his better known songs, people are in a near frenzy, jiving and jumping about. It's good for me too, I lie, smiling as he sings Coo Ca Choo. I wondered if in different circumstances I would even be there at all. My potentially good place now feels like a trap and I am helpless to change the situation.

I have to admire his performance but like one of his songs, "I Wish It Was Yesterday" - I wonder if he does too…

Thankfully my former lady colleagues had adapted well to me being in a wheelchair. After all it had had an effect on them as well and some of them were still riding… Whoever took me to a party or dinner out (be it Janet, Joan, Michelle or Carey - sometimes with husbands) knew that Gee Armytage, one of my former colleagues, or even one of the boys could cope if I needed assistance. The camaraderie that jockeys share never dies. I was still 'Shazza' to them and the wheelchair would never change that. Then of course there was also the strength of my friendship with Richard Phillips, who had been an almost constant companion at the Jockey's events since my return home.

As I reflect now I am lucky to have had so many brilliant times! One Christmas party, held at the Sudbury House Hotel in Farringdon, was a fantastic do. I had all my old buddies on the same table - Gee, Lorna Vincent and Jacqui Oliver, the table number made up with some of the boys. Far from being embarrassed and pushed in a corner just to observe, reminisce and maybe feel sorry that I wasn't the one up there dancing, I was back in the fold - weighed in!

I was pleased when Jo Lodder took the time to come and sit with me. We had a long chat which was pleasant. He complimented me on my overall appearance and trimness. He would never realise how crucial those words were - for I was still at a stage when I had lost confidence with my body image.

Richard appeared from the dance floor and said he was whacked - it was only 2.30am! He asked me if I wanted him to get Janet or Joan but Jo assured him that he would take good care of me. We said goodnight and Richard was gone.

I'd always loved to dance and my friends knew that - but I was far removed from being envious because I wanted them to enjoy their lives for I knew how easily it could be all taken away. I'm upset if they are discontented with their lot - as I once was - but I was ebullient that night and along with Graham Bradley (Brad), his girlfriend (now wife) Amanda (Bob) and Belinda Tory we sang, and they waved their arms in the air as I paddled one of mine to 'Walking on Sunshine'. The sheer beauty of the scene was that instinctively they remained sitting down.

This was the company where Shazza could let her hair down!

I received a letter and some photos a couple of weeks later from Jacqui Oliver - you cannot imagine my horror when they revealed (and the camera never lies) that, in fact, sitting in-between Brad and Bob (part-time model) was a round faced, curly permed, big haired, Shirley Valentine look-alike! I definitely had a sense of humour failure that day. The sight repulsed me.

Whoever Jo saw on that night was very different to the person that faced me. I was hardly eating anything, but when I did it was the wrong kind of food. I didn't eat sweet things anymore either, luckily those taste nerves must have been severed. A dietician came to see me and she confirmed what I already knew. I needed to cut down on calories and cut down mostly on the red wine (my painkiller). My unit intake was between six and eight every evening, more if I went out at night or Sunday lunch, was something she didn't need to know, after the recommended amount was written down!

I had been on a diet most of my life but I couldn't waste like before by running in a sweat suit or eating only one boiled egg and half a grapefruit twice a day for nearly a week without exercise. I was having physio three times a week then as well, and one of those sessions was swimming. I started to diet but I would fail miserably.

The Lesters - the jockeys' equivalent of the BAFTA Awards - has become the highlight of my social calendar. I was invited in 1992 to enjoy myself which I did immensely (the original It Girl on wheels), then in 1995 I presented Lord Oaksey with an award for his services to the Injured Jockeys' Fund. I'd heard once that people perceive you as 70% what you look like, 20% what you sound like and only 10% of what you say - so if you look good and sound good nobody really takes a lot of notice of what you say!

Visually, I had to pull out all the stops for that night! I came home from Cambridge with a long black velvet dress, enhanced by a small diamante clasp that held a long flowing chiffon scarf. I needed the beautician, the hairdresser, the image artist - God, I needed the works! I would be centre stage, in front of 900 people (including former colleagues), during the presentation. I looked at myself in the carefully placed mirror in my bedroom, "You look lovely," Janet said, to which I replied, "I need to lose weight". I felt like a whale... The compliments were interpreted as kindness until the champagne kicked in and then I partied as hard as the rest of them!

The year after, I needed the champagne before we set off! Helen, my beautician who has now become a good friend, put my make-up on by the light of the window, so I didn't see my face until it was all finished. Result - not happy, I looked like a tart. She assured me that by the evening light it wouldn't look so over the top, I wasn't convinced but it was time to set off. I could just about manage to hook my hand under the sun visor in the car and look in the mirror. I must have looked in it about half a dozen times before we'd reached Royston (not far away from Newmarket) when Sian Farmer (nee Day, a friend who accompanied me on a few occasions) asked, "Has it worn off yet?" Needless to say it was all right by the evening.

I was very excited about my next London trip, as we were to stay the night in a top hotel. An easy task for me to organise and I booked two rooms on the same floor through a Reservations Agency in my name. A double for my friends Andy Young (who runs his livery and eventing stables behind my bungalow), his wife, Dawn, and a twin for Michelle and myself so she would be able to attend to me if I needed assistance during the night. I had specified my needs and informed them I was in a wheelchair. I think the best way of relaying my experience is by the letters written, received - but not fully understood! I rang the Reservation Agency informing them of my proposed letter, they were most helpful and supportive and requested a copy.

29th March 1997

Dear Sir,

I am writing to express my dissatisfaction at the service provided by your staff both on my arrival at, and my stay in, your hotel on Sunday 23rd March.

Having booked rooms in advance and making clear that I am confined to a wheelchair, you can imagine my reaction to finding that my booking for one twin room and one double room on the same floor had not been met. I was offered, after a protracted discussion, two double rooms on the same floor as an alternative. It must have been clear to your duty staff that I am not in a position to share a bed with my helper. It was quite distressing for me to have to insist on accommodation as booked. This was finally offered. Subsequently I was asked for an additional payment of £20 for my room which I quite understandably refused, as the booking error was not my responsibility.

Your staff insisted upon full payment before they would give us the door pass cards. I have not experienced this in any other hotel I have stayed in. I explained I would be making a cash payment, but that my purse was in one of my cases. To my great embarrassment your staff were insistent and the case had to be opened in full view of a lobby full of people.

When I requested that a taxi converted for wheelchair access be called I again, I am afraid, found your staff wanting, although such a cab was finally summoned.

In conclusion I wish to draw to your attention the helpful and pleasant night porter, who gave me every assistance when I returned from the function I had attended, in the early hours. This was in marked contrast to my earlier experience and was much appreciated.

Yours faithfully,

In response to this I received the following:

2nd April 1997

Dear Miss Murgatroyd,

Thank you for your recent letter, I am very sorry that you have had cause to complain following your recent stay. I was appalled to read of your experiences and have made it clear to the front of house manager that such insensitive behaviour by her staff is not acceptable.

In view of your unsatisfactory experiences, I would like to offer you a complimentary night's accommodation to include English breakfast on a date of your choice, subject to availability. This may be combined, if you wish, with a further night at a special rate of £33 per person again inclusive of breakfast. This offer is open for the next twelve months and I would be grateful if you will make the booking through my office so that I may make the necessary arrangements.

Thank you once again for bringing this matter to our attention, without your letter I would have been unable to take the positive action which has now improved our level of service.

Yours sincerely,

I then received the following from the Reservation Agency:

4th April 1997

Dear Miss Murgatroyd,

Thank you for forwarding me a copy of your letter to the xxx Hotel expressing your dissatisfaction with the service you received whilst staying there. It is very important to us as a company that these matters are brought to our attention.

As soon as I received your letter I contacted the General Manager, who could not apologise enough for the embarrassment caused to you when you checked in, and he has copied me the letter he has personally sent to you.

On behalf of my organisation I would also like to apologise for the embarrassment and inconvenience caused to you during your stay. I hope we may be able to look after your hotel needs in the future and will do everything in our power to ensure that this situation does not arise again.

If I can be of any further assistance then please do not hesitate to contact me.

Kind regards.

I was satisfied that this gesture went some way towards compensating us over our stay. By sheer coincidence I had been asked by the Spinal Injuries Association to appear in and voice-over a video they were putting together called 'Feel Fit'. Their aim was to show a level of exercise even for tetraplegics. It was to take place in London and I could accept the offer of the complimentary discount from the hotel.

I rang the Reservation Agency and informed them I would like to stay for two nights. I requested adjoining rooms, as Michelle and her husband would accompany me. I was assured that this time it would be no problem ... (we are talking top hotel here).

We arrived in London at 8.30pm where the video was going to be filmed and I immediately telephoned the hotel advising them we would be arriving in approximately an hour, before running through the tight itinerary of the next two days. So far - so good.

At around 9.45pm we entered the hotel only to find that I was on Floor 4 and my helpers were on Floor 2. "Pardon"? This was the reservation we had made, the assistant manager informed Michelle, who was standing behind me - thus completely overlooking my presence. "Excuse me," I said politely - "I am the one who booked the accommodation, it was booked through the manager." I asked for him, to which she retorted, "He isn't here, he is at home, he does have to sleep sometimes!" Her general attitude was beyond comprehension. There ensued a raising of voices to which (and I am not proud of this) I blurted "I need my sleep as well, I have to be up to shoot a video in the morning"!

So you can imagine, things were getting quite heated, when another lady appeared obviously sent to calm the situation. Looking at the reservations on the computer she could find no alternative, she advised us, but to book us into another hotel and could we wait in the bar where she would inform us as to the new arrangements? I thanked her for being helpful and said that the drinks would obviously be complimentary, wouldn't they? Naturally.

A taxi arrived and took us to our new destination - surroundings plush, ramps visible but unobtrusive. We arrived at the desk, and Michelle handed the charming concierge the correspondence from the previous hotel outlining our situation; again there were some whisperings and tapping away on computers. As midnight approached the concierge requested £200 deposit and informed us that this excluded breakfast unless we would like to pay a further £10 each! Good job I was sitting down.

"No", I replied, explaining it wasn't up to me to provide the deposit; after all it was a complimentary stay inclusive of breakfast. We were asked if we would like to take a seat in the foyer. Still smiling (I think not) we waited patiently even though, by now, we were quite tired. After a short time we were shown to our rooms, but unfortunately the plush disabled room with double bed was at the opposite end of the corridor to the other twin bedded room! Too tired to dispute any longer, Michelle's husband stayed in the disabled room and we took the twin room...

On my return home I told the Reservation Agency's director (by now we were on first name terms) about the palaver - he listened in disbelief - and then I wrote the following:

22nd May 1997

Dear Jonathan,

Thank you for all your help and understanding over my experiences at the xxx Hotel.

It is unfortunate that in our world of such great technology, some able-bodied human specimens still find it so hard to keep up with the treatment of a wheelchair-bound person. They cannot quite comprehend that there is a difference between being physically 'HANDICAPPED' and mentally 'HANDICAPPED'. I wonder if their short sightedness, yet another 'HANDICAP' is brought on by them becoming power-struck at the label on their lapel which reads 'Ass istant Manager'. Oh dear, I made a typing error - it must be something to do with my wheelchair!

Now I'm not one to complain, as you well know Jonathan! But where were the staff of a certain London hotel on December 4th last year when an act was passed in Parliament, the title being 'Disability Awareness'. All businesses were instructed to treat everyone in the same way, whether they had wheels instead of legs or white sticks instead of eyes. Obviously some just turned a deaf ear; that old 'HANDICAP' keeps cropping up!!

I have enclosed a few fliers of my recently published book called

'Jump Jockeys Don't Cry'. I will leave it to your own discretion as to where you distribute them, no doubt some will find their way into the hands of a certain Hotel.

Ironically, when I rode in jump races, I used to like the horses that were well 'HANDICAPPED'!

Kind regards.

So, this was yet another bad experience of trying to lead a normal life whilst being in a wheelchair. I understand there are many able-bodied people who state special requirements before arrival at a hotel and as far as I was concerned I was just another customer who had certain needs.

Since then I have stayed in many hotels and the service has been excellent. I'd like to be able to say that everybody is now treating wheelchair users as if they have not got the plague but unfortunately some are still left wanting! Understandably, the next year I asked Janet to drive us home so we didn't have to stay overnight in a hotel!

The Lesters again proved to be a night of magic. Richard Phillips and I, in a particularly mischievous mood, amused ourselves dodging Sian by joyriding in the Hilton lift! I was still in 'high spirits' or was it high on spirits? Can't remember - anyway I persuaded Richard and Sian, with the help of someone I called 'My Lester Buddy', sadly the now late Sara Hood, to follow the other jockeys who were making their way to another hotel. We hailed a (disabled) taxi and took off into the sharp London night - well...early hours of the morning to be precise (much to Janet's chagrin - not because we had gone but because we didn't tell her). On this occasion she had waited in Richard's room ready to drive us home. Janet enquired as to our whereabouts at 3am and was told by a doorman that "Yes, a girl in a wheelchair had left the building"!

When we finally arrived back about 7am I fancied a stroll in the streets of London but Richard was having none of it. As always I did not want the revelry to end but he needed his bed and needed me to get in my car and head back to Newmarket pronto! I promised to tell Janet in future if I expected my night and day to become one. I also knew that the drinking was getting out of order. I ignored it - I could cut down any time I liked. The drink took away the physical pain and I was making the most of every opportunity I was handed; and anyway I didn't eat a lot.

I always saw Graham Bradley (Brad) at those uplifting Lester Award nights but the poignancy was always there. Brad was one of the jockeys who waited anxiously outside the ambulance room after my fall. When I had my body protector removed I let out a chilling scream. This was too much for him and the next moment he appeared at the foot of the plinth full of concern. I told him, "I'm alright, just broken both shoulders and collar bones," and he left, satisfied. He told me later that it was a big shock when the subsequent prognosis was far worse. Each year we had the same conversation, he always asked if I remembered - and I always replied "Yes".

I had only spoken to Brad a couple of times prior to my accident; I remember the first instance his emotions struck me were when we gathered to say farewell to our former boss Tony Dickinson. The boss's funeral was in Gisburn where I had worked but I hadn't moved on to Harewood (where Brad later joined them).

I have found that over the years his continued concern has been both flattering and appreciated. Maybe this is why the Hilton foyer (after the Lesters) was witness to a very emotional scene following a happy and drink-fuelled evening. Richard Dunwoody and Brad were saying their goodbyes to me with hugs and kisses, then Brad, dear Brad, became so emotional he set us all off. I can't really remember what was said or how it even started but I told him, in a breaking voice - "Jump Jockeys Don't Cry". The next moment I was in the car on my way home and it was the first time I cried - no, I didn't cry, I sobbed my heart out. I missed my former life so much. I missed the horses, the racing and all the boys who had never ostracised me - I hadn't been treated as a loose cannon.

Janet drove in silence and Sian tried to help by saying - "Jump Jockeys Don't Cry". "I'm not a jump jockey any more," I lamented… I went straight to bed when we arrived home. I could still smell their aftershave as I drifted off to sleep. The incident was never mentioned again - until now. Richard phoned next day and asked, "What happened to you last night?" Evasively I replied, "Nothing, why?" He had wondered where I'd sloped off to without saying goodnight to him. I hadn't said goodnight to Richard…

To recap, the first time I met Richard properly was in April 1992 at a fund-raising event for my benefit. He is a very talented impersonator and often the entertainment at any racing party.

As a thank you for all their help over the past year, I decided to treat Janet, Jill (Delaney), Petra and my dear friend Ali Thom to a night out at the Amateur Riders Ball in February 1993. Ali drove and was none too pleased when we arrived in Newbury and couldn't locate the hotel - she then had to telephone from a 'phone box for the right directions. Even then we were given the wrong ones. This led to yet another stop for further enquiries - the night was not looking too good for me as everyone presumed I knew exactly where we were going! I broke a short silence with, "Well, I wonder who will be the first to pull tonight?" Ali's retort was, "The two grannies in the back (meaning Janet and Jill) have no chance. Neither have you because you're a crip and that only leaves Petra (tall, blonde Swedish beauty) and myself. Petra's 6 to 4 on and I'm 7 to 2...and drifting." The gauntlet was thrown!

The Ball was held in a marquee at the rear of the hotel (remember, this was February and it transpired to be too cold even for polar bears) and the only form of heating was one gas Superser. We sat at our table and my friends kept their coats on while I gamely took mine off. "It's not that cold, is it?" - I tried to make light of the so far joyless evening. At last, after what seemed an eternity, the food was ready and, to add insult to injury, it was a cold buffet ...

So when the auction started, hosted by Richard, they would probably have preferred to go home. I suggested we just stayed for this entertainment and then leave. The auction was going well when a pair of tickets for a weekend in London came up for bidding. By circling the floor Richard raised the bidding to £250; I beckoned him over and said cheekily (slightly inebriated to keep out the cold), "I'll go to £300 if they include you!" He returned to his podium, banged his gavel and shouted "Sold to Sharron Murgatroyd". Striding back to me he said with a smile, "We'll have a really good time". I turned quick as a flash and announced, "I've pulled!"

As we prepared to leave Richard told me that I'd had a right result - Richard Dunwoody had unexpectedly picked up the tab for the tickets. I told him I must say thank you straight away as he really shouldn't have paid for our tickets. "He hasn't paid for our tickets, he's only paid for yours!"

Petra and her boyfriend Robin accompanied me when the weekend in London came round. It was slightly awkward on arrival at the hotel but Richard seemed unfazed about us sharing the twin bedded room, leaving the double for the other two. We had a stroll around Hyde Park and I chatted a lot, no surprise there, and his natural easy manner with me was refreshing. We shared the same bizarre sense of humour and basically had fun. If this had been a date under normal circumstances you would think it was going well but I was under no illusion. I had already resigned myself to a life that would never include another person.

After we'd all been out for dinner and were returning to the hotel he asked a road sweeper with cart, broom and shovel if he'd like to swap, pushing me towards a (not at all amused) cleaner of the highway! "I'm not that bad when you get to know me"; even this did not amuse him - whilst the rest of us roared.

There are numerous things in my life that can never be the same and I was about to realise one of the most fundamental. Fortunately the people who were my helpers and friends made the fact that I was going to share a room with someone of the opposite sex less of an issue. After a couple of hours sleep I awoke, nothing unusual there. I could hear the rain and noise of the London traffic below and Richard's steady breathing, and questioned my very being there. Was this right or wrong? I mean it wasn't as if we were in the same bed. Did anybody care? All I knew was that it was strangely comforting for me.

I hoped the rain would soon stop as Richard had suggested we go to Covent Garden in the morning, he particularly mentioned the spectacle of the jugglers. Although it seemed an age before morning arrived, Richard slept soundly (OK for some) and when he eventually awoke I told him it had been raining all night and questioned whether we were still going to see the jugglers. He queried why - and I said innocently, "Well, they might not be performing because their balls will be slippery". A well known phrase was borne from this as he joked, "You just think you are so funny, don't you?" I replied, "Yes, and it's your turn to get up and make the tea!" Situation solved.

After that I soon realised I had a crush on Richard for a while but I certainly wasn't going to jeopardise my friendship with him by admitting it. His early training days saw some tough times with bad or frustrating horses and I liked it when he 'phoned me to talk about them. Sometimes I said, "If only I could muck out and ride a few." "I need help not hindrance," came the reply and we'd end up going into nonsensical patter and laughter; it seemed to lighten the load.

He was especially interested in what I was doing and I kept him up to speed about selling my books and practising my carriage driving in the horse and trap. I had started carriage driving after meeting a lady called Sue Ram. I gave it a go and liked it, so then every Thursday afternoon I went driving. With the promise of competition (when I became more adept with my new sport) I enthusiastically began to learn the right skills. I loved bending round the cones (at speed), manoeuvring in and out of the woods during the cross country phase, finishing by going through the gate (at speed) but I'm afraid I couldn't get to grips with the dressage due to my uncooperative right arm and, at times, a less than enthusiastic horse. Richard started calling me Ben Hur. "How many books have you sold today, Ben Hur?" "Two and the story is priceless," I say...

It was a drizzly Thursday for my weekly excursion to the horse and trap and Janet agreed it looked like a waterproof job. We were waiting for a man who was coming to watch me driving with interest. I heard a knock at the front door.

"Janet, I think he's here."

Janet immediately invited him in and ushered him into my office where I was waiting. I had my back to the doorway and she told him he would have to face me, as I couldn't turn round. I greeted him with a cheery smile, noticing he had an unusually thick briefcase type of bag. New technology I thought.

"Hi, where would you like me?"

He looked bemused.

"Well, where would you like to start?"

"Are you expecting somebody else?" he asked.

I said, "You are the photographer, aren't you?"

"No, I'm a Jehovah's Witness."

I shouted, "Janet, you've only let a bloody Jehovah's Witness in!"

My impertinence gave me a great result; I sold him a book and he just happened to be a computer buff who showed me how to solve a small glitch with one of my programs! His name was Brett and his thick briefcase was not for a new slimline camera, just a load of free booklets. He thanked us as he left - it was the warmest welcome he had ever received!

There was another knock at the door - this time it was the photographer; and another book was sold!

So it was a pleasure to be there when Richard ('Richie') trained his first flat winner Queens Cottage - apt as she was half sister to Beechwood Cottage who had been a mainstay for trainer Alan Bailey when I was his assistant and a long time after that. I had won two races on him and was placed on numerous occasions.

Our friendship now is one of ease, he stays at Becklyn whenever there are any functions, sales or racing at Newmarket. He has a key and this hospitality is a reciprocal arrangement. When guests were invited to Derek Thompson's evening wedding reception he rang me to say that in addition to himself was it okay if Michael Caulfield and John Francome came to watch England v Spain European Cup '96 in the afternoon. "Yes, of course that will be alright." "Good, I've already invited them!"

John 'phoned to ask whether or not I would like fish and chips. No, I didn't eat at lunchtimes "You don't know what you are missing," he exclaimed. When they all descended on me, they proceeded to rearrange my sitting-room furniture - settee as close to the television as possible, coffee table for their pots of tea - and I was told by the three of them not to speak whilst the football was on! Amused, I drank the beers that they had previously declined.

It was like watching telly with three loud 11-year-olds! With gasps of disbelief they shouted at the players - "Oh, what is he doing!", "Did you see that?". Then a brief discussion about the way they had all played so well the previous Sunday.

"I thought we weren't allowed to speak whilst the football was on…"

"You're not"! they said in unison.

I honestly used to loathe football but since then I must admit I have been converted. We shared an afternoon of fun followed by a terrific night out - what more can a girl ask for?

On one occasion when Richard was staying overnight he returned late and, thinking I might still be awake, he came into my room but found me sound asleep. In the morning he told me this and, as my inspiration for poetry comes from many different sources, I wrote the following poem 'Sleeping Free'.

Sleeping Free

Caught me sleeping last night
Softly stepped into my room but I was oblivious to you.
Soaring in my night flight
Where dreams are good
You saw me - sleeping free.

Watched me sleeping last night
My hand was there for you to hold but you were oblivious
To my aching soul.
Walking in our different worlds,
This was me - sleeping free.

Left me sleeping last night
In my hours of peace and calm gently breathing pain away.
In readiness for another day
When laughter masks a thousand words
Look at me - sleeping free.

Leave me in my sleeping night
Stroke my hair without a commitment for life.
And we can share a moment in time
In my darkened cave that's so alive,
Hope for me - sleeping free.

CHAPTER FOUR

MAR-Y-SOL
BLISS TINGED WITH SADNESS

When the former jump jockey turned trainer, Jack Berry's son, Sam, bought an apartment at Mar-Y-Sol in Tenerife to help his recovery through the winter months, I suppose he never reckoned on arranging a trip to help others. Sam, aged 20, lay in a coma for a month after his hurdle race fall at Sedgefield in 1985 where he sustained a severe head injury. Jack saw how the warmth and pleasant surroundings of the Mar-Y-Sol complex enhanced his son's recovery.

As we have found, the racing fraternity always pulls together in a crisis or anybody else's crisis. Witness Philip Mitchell and the Bosnia trip (when he organised a convoy of horse boxes loaded with all sorts of different items for the refugees). The open day held at Jack Berry's Cockerham stables in August '92, was to raise money to send other injured jockeys for a holiday in the sun. Thanks to Jack and his staff, on a cold February morning in 1993, myself and seven others were in the airport lounge at Luton - destination Los Cristianos...

I must admit when I was first asked if I would like to go on this holiday, I was slightly apprehensive. I don't think I had bottled out of anything before but I would not have needed much of an excuse to stay locked away in my home, cosy by the log fire. No viable reason could be found. So here I was now, looking forward to my first holiday since my own fall in a hurdle race at Bangor-on-Dee, the result of which had left me paralysed.

Just days less than a year after my release from Oswestry Orthopaedic Hospital lots of thoughts went through my mind. Was I ready to go on holiday? Would my companions and I be able to cope? Is it feasible for wheelchair-bound people to go abroad? All these questions were soon to be answered - but not without a few setbacks.

Although very uncomfortable in the aeroplane seat, the flight was the same as any other I had been on previously. On arrival at Tenerife airport, two hurrying locals desperately manhandled me from seat to makeshift wheelchair. I felt ominously like a sack of potatoes with my uncontrollable legs bumping against each side of the aisle seats. My companions' voices were at near fever pitch telling them to "Be careful!" but the only response they received was a few gibberish sounds ending with the word, "Que?" All warnings I had been given 'to be careful' were cast aside in one fell swoop.

"Uno momento," Manuel One said as he parked me outside the aircraft, slumped in the seat with my dignity slipping away. So to lighten my situation as my companions anxiously looked on, I imagined John Cleese appearing shouting orders at me, "Come on then, get out of that chair! You can't? Okay then, right, right". Then he would turn round and slap Manuel for his bad manners. Amidst the faces obviously worried that I would sink into a sulky mood, I decided I would not let the ignorance of Manuel One or Two upset me, even when Manuel One began to insist that I sit on a plastic moulded seat in the airport lounge whilst waiting for my own wheelchair. But instead of becoming irate at my predicament, I stayed calm in the face of adversity and as I was pushed out to face the brilliant sunshine, no Manuel was going to spoil my holiday:

"QUE...?"

That was my first experience of travelling as a wheelchair jockey. Over the years it has become better - although every now and again we come across a know-all 'Jobsworth' who is the one out of three people who think everyone on wheels is below average intelligence! Fact.

This type of holiday was very much a distant dream for Jack Berry as he had realised before his son was born that there would be many jockeys crippled in mind or body - as they pursued the euphoria of winning.

The 1964 Grand National on March 21st saw Jack's comrade and popular northern jockey, Paddy Farrell, take a backbreaking fall at the Chair fence on 'Border Flight' in front of the packed grandstand. Paddy was paralysed from the waist down. The possibility of such an injury happening had been harbouring in the minds of riders for far too long. It was time for an immediate plan of action. This was a second reminder, as only three months before on December 4th, the hugely popular and fearless Tim Brookshaw had suffered the same injury over hurdles on 'Lucky Dora', also at Liverpool. Brookshaw had been champion jockey in the 1958/'59 season but his riding of 'Wyndburgh' in the 1959 Grand National was one of the greatest exhibitions of horsemanship witnessed at the time. A broken stirrup leather at Bechers on the second circuit would not stop him - he rode the rest of the awesome course without any stirrups! He was only beaten by one and half-lengths by 'Oxo'.

A public appeal to set up a fund was made for the two stricken jockeys. The love of racing and compassion for the jockeys' plight generated some very generous universal donations. Jockeys who were still riding targeted the bookmakers from north to south. This whole 'plan of action' became a united effort.

A band of trustees was formed. The Chairman of the trustees was

Clifford Nicholson, a wealthy Lincolnshire land and racehorse owner. Farrell had ridden his first winner at Roscommon on 'Port Luna' owned by Nicholson and on New Year's Day 1953 his win on 'Sontogo' cemented the relationship between owner and jockey. When 'Sontogo' set sail on the Dublin to Liverpool ferry to join Nicholson's other Irish graduates trained by Charlie Hall, near Tadcaster, Farrell soon joined him.

The other trustees included Edward Courage CBE, owner and trainer of 'Border Flight'. He knew all too well what the two jockeys faced - he had been struck down by polio in his early 30s and confined to life in a wheelchair. The others were four times champion jockey, Fred Winter CBE, who had hung up his boots after the Cheltenham Festival that same year; Wing Commander PDO Vaux and The Honourable John Lawrence, one of the top flight amateur riders at the time and journalist for The Telegraph. A progress report issued in 1967 states that these men were the initial trustees.

Three times champion jockey Stan Mellor was acting as a liaison officer between the fund and the southern committee of The Professional National Hunt Jockey's Association (Great Britain) of which he was Chairman, and Major Peter Smith TD became the Secretary. The amalgamation of these owners, trainers and jockeys played a pivotal role - between them they took over the reins to manage the overwhelming response of the public. A private trust named 'The Farrell-Brookshaw Fund' was born.

This fund soon rollercoasted beyond anyone's expectations. It became obvious, as donations soared, that the welfare of Farrell and Brookshaw was guaranteed. With their consent in April of the same year the fund was closed and further monies were used to set up a registered charity called 'The Injured National Hunt Jockeys' Fund'.

Understandably there were many kind hands that helped in those early days. Stan Mellor - a great friend of Brookshaw, as Jack Berry was of Farrell - visited and helped other injured jockeys in aid of the fund.

It wasn't until 1969 that Sue Mills was appointed the first 'Almoner', undertaking this work in a voluntary capacity. Her job was to visit the 18 injured people of that time, offering both financial and caring support, which has become an integral part of the fund. The report back to the trustees could then determine the type of input needed. The rapport between almoner and injured can make all the difference towards enhancing recovery by easing certain pressures of life.

As time went by it also became apparent that flat jockeys were taking some life-threatening falls. The trustees approached the Charity Commissioners with a view to include all jockeys. In 1971 the fund became 'The Injured Jockeys' Fund'. Upon the death of Edward Courage in 1982, the former John Lawrence (who had been known as Lord Oaksey since 1970) took over as Chairman. Fred Winter retired as a trustee in 1991, leaving Lord Oaksey as the only founder member.

There have obviously been various trustees (and almoners) throughout the years who have given their time, support and ideas without payment and all must be highly praised. For 27 years Bob McCreery, an ex-amateur rider, breeder and businessman, served the Fund as a trustee and on his retirement at the end of the millennium, that year's calendar was just one testament of his achievements.

The ultimate accolade has to be for Lord Oaksey - the man who, for 37 years, has worked tirelessly in the name of the charity. In 1964 the trustees came up the innovative idea of having Christmas cards of racing scenes, available for people to buy. The first was titled 'Four Great Chasers' painted by Peter Beigel, depicting 'Arkle' (Pat Taaffe), 'Mill House' (Willie Robinson), 'Passeul' (Dave Dick) and 'Kings Nephew' (Stan Mellor). Whilst working for The Telegraph the then John Lawrence, arranged for staff to deal with orders. These cards have been boosting revenue ever since. Courageously, on the eve of his 65th birthday, egged on by the Channel Four Racing Team, he did a bungee jump at Uttoxeter races, once more going beyond the call of duty for the IJF. He has travelled the country to make after-dinner speeches, teatime speeches and, for all we know, probably even morning speeches! He is not only known as 'The Noble Lord' but as the assiduous Trustee and Chairman - he is the modest 'Mr IJF'.

At present there are about 800 beneficiaries on the books. Some of these have enjoyed at least one holiday - some have declined for whatever reason. I have been fortunate to have shared many holidays with some wonderful people who, but for a quirk of fate, I might never have met at all.

It must have been particularly satisfying for Jack to see his old colleague Paddy Farrell (the Irishman who in the autumn of 1953 he befriended on arrival at Charlie Hall's Towton Stables) enjoy many holidays at Mar-Y-Sol before he passed away in 1999.

This first holiday was very much an experiment - bringing former jockeys of various ages and injury time-scales together might have been disastrous. It could have been seen as a way for some to face that they were now disabled and had to be with others who were. Most of us had returned to our former life in or around the racing community and still hadn't mixed with other disabled people. It may have been perceived as a realisation that a once fit, athletic body was now being labelled - before the head had time to acknowledge it!

With racing as the common denominator and two men to set an

example - Jimmy Harris and Jonathan Haynes - this was one 'Titanic Trip' that would not flounder. We were all racing people and that bravado blood isn't washed out easily, if at all. The late Jimmy Harris - jump jockey turned trainer after breaking his back at Huntingdon in 1971 - had provided me with many rides. He was a 'no nonsense trainer' and gave me my first ride in the prestigious Diamond race at Ascot. I never thought he was different to any other trainer. I never saw him as disabled but I did see sadness in his eyes when he and his wife Ann visited me in hospital. It was an awful shock to be told he had died on 30th June 2001.

Ironically, Jonathan Haynes was working for Jimmy Harris when he took an outside ride at Southwell in 1980, aged 20 - his horse flipped over, pinning him to the ground. He was dragged out with a broken back. He had never been on holiday until now but was well adjusted to his situation and took great pride in his appearance.

The rest of us all met at a relatively early stage of our new life and all needed help with eating and drinking, but over the years we have become stronger in mind and body. People like: Lee Davis, 19 when a car crash left him with a broken neck, finishing his promising career in the saddle; Andrew James, 33 when he suffered a broken neck in a Hunter Chase at Ludlow only 2 months before my fall; Jenny Liston, at 30 a very successful point-to-point rider who had suffered a head injury which had not only curbed her mobility but also affected her speech badly - much the same as Sam Berry.

The older members included the aforementioned Paddy Farrell who was a quiet, softly spoken Irishman. When he was asked if he'd like to go in the pool, he confessed that he could not swim before his accident, so he didn't see how he would stay afloat now! However he reluctantly agreed to have a go. Paddy Broderick (twice winner of the Champion Hurdle on 'Night Nurse') and his wife Nan, were his chief helpers and soon he was floating round with them supporting his head and shoulders. After that he really came alive and loved going in the therapeutic pool.

Ronnie Singer, the 19-year-old champion flat apprentice jockey had been unseated at the start of the 1960 Liverpool Spring Cup - after three furlongs he hit the ground again. He lay in a coma for three months, his career over before it had hardly started. The 52-year-old man has full mobility but a vague memory of his life since his fall.

There may have been a few worried faces (not injured jockeys) amongst the almoners and trustees every now and again but the trip was deemed a success - not least because of the input of the now retired almoner Hilary Kerr. Since then the IJF have continued, with the help of Jack Berry, to send at least 50 beneficiaries to Tenerife once a year.

There is an undying camaraderie that is the essence of this sport -

where dreams are fulfilled whilst others are snuffed out - where the lucky ones don't just stand and stare.

The Sporting Life asked me to write a report on one of the Injured Jockeys' Fund's holidays, and the following is the original piece:

MAR-Y-SOL
Bliss Tinged With Sadness
February 1995

Where do I begin to tell the story of how sweet life can be? Even when faced with adversity there is still a lot of life to live and the Injured Jockeys' Trip to Tenerife once again proved that. With the help of Jack Berry, the instigator of these trips, funds were made available for the third year running. A party of 53 people, including helpers and almoners, were flown for a holiday in the sun... to enjoy!
I made this trip 2 years ago somewhat apprehensively, as I know others did this year, but now being an experienced wheelchair jockey I looked forward to it with relish. As the plane left cold, windy Luton, destination Los Cristianos, I was already anticipating the sun on my face. Once airborne I contentedly sipped at my Buck's Fizz, safe in the knowledge that on arrival, my two lady helpers would block any attempts by the scurrying local porters to manhandle me from plane seat to makeshift wheelchair, as had previously happened.

Slipping easily into holiday spirit, we re-acquainted ourselves with surroundings and the other members of our party. Winter woollies were soon exchanged for swimsuits and sarongs, cup-a-soup for long cool beers and within a few days inhibitions were discarded. Our riding careers may have come to an untimely end but as I sat in the company of Dai Tegg, Gareth Charles-Jones, Jonathan Haynes, Peter Dun, Lee Davis and Barbara Towler - I know we still have plenty to offer. Although sometimes we don't realise this, when our own pain is the only pain we feel...
There is a lot of living to do and if the laughter had been monitored on those clear warm nights, it would surely have shot off the Richter scale!

The opportunity to swim every day in a warm pool under blazing sunshine was very therapeutic. The aches and pains were soon soothed away, mentally and physically. Maybe only shelved for a while but away they would stay at least until the end of this holiday. Some of us could not quite manage to swim on our own, unless arms and legs were trussed up in water wings and neck brace was fitted, but for those who could the joy was clearly seen. I only ventured out once like this as I told my helper Janet, "I feel like a dinghy." With that all aids came off and with her holding me only by my shoulders and head, I moved both arms to float and also felt light and free. We watched Fred Winter dive down for coins under the watchful eye of his wife and when retrieved his smile and laughter were yet another bridge crossed, another challenge conquered.

There were a wide variety of night-time activities. Some of the retired jockeys who had not met for over 20 years chatted about the old days. The card game Uno produced plenty of wild shrieks and accusations of cheating, all unfounded of course! Jenga was also popular and if you were feeling really brave you could always go to Las Americas with the boys (already mentioned plus a few more) but there was the small worry of not all returning together...if at all!

High Spirits and High Morale

The game Jenga was a big source of entertainment, in turn everyone removed a wooden block from any part of the made-up tower and replaced it on top. The only rule being, to use one hand. The grandstand jockeys came out in force, myself included, telling the players which block to go for. The shakier the tower became the more instructions, mostly from Jeremy Richardson in his officious solicitor's voice. Hilary Kerr, the northern almoner, told him to put his hands where his mouth was but he declined. Unfortunately, the lady players, fed up with his badgering, were unable to catch him and push him in the pool after the last game!

Our night out at what is known as the Pig Farm (the biggest pork chops you have ever seen) was certainly an evening to remember. We sat down on one long table, all 53 of us. It was Jonathan Haynes' birthday, Jack Berry recited one of his funny poems and everyone who liked the vino tinto were pretty well legless (sorry)! It also brought to light the high spirits of the evening before. Andy Williams, who is Lee Davis' friend and helper, not the singer, was the victim of this prank. He woke up to find they had shaved off his eyebrow. From now on I told him you will be known as 'One Eyebrow', and like some of the others who acquired nicknames he didn't mind.

Noel Boston and Linda O'Hara were regularly on 'towel and sunbed duty'; the Swedes, in this case, didn't stand a chance, let alone the odd German. I wonder what they say about us! We only wanted about 20 together anyway… My sunbathing place next to Jimmy Harris, Johnny (Lightning) O'Hara, their wives Ann and Linda (when not shopping at the market) and my two ladies, Janet and Joan, was where I held on-the-spot 'Live in Tenerife' interviews. The answers were mostly the same, as were the questions. It was unanimous; everybody was having a great time! My chat with Nancy Stephenson was cut short as she had been invited to a lunch party. She was very pleased as it was her birthday. It turned out that the party was being held in an apartment just behind us. She pointed it out. "But that's my apartment," I said, surprised. Peter Dun and Noel (Norman) Boston laid out lunch and wine and we crammed as many people in as we could. It was wonderful and the first of three parties that day for Nancy.

The informal speeches on the last night were both funny and emotional. We are forever grateful to the trustees and almoners of the I.J.F. Our sport embracing us, never turning away and as Jimmy Uttley said, "If we cannot enjoy ourselves, it has to be our own fault".

The camaraderie of Mar-Y-Sol was The Bliss…The Sadness…the reason we were here in the first place and that we all had to say, "Adios Amigos".

In February '96 there was a bit of ducking and diving going on in Mar-Y-Sol. The reason was that Channel Four Racing were sending out a film crew to promote and raise awareness of how beneficial the holiday had proved to be for young and old former jockeys. Director Stephen Burn could be spotted in corners or high up on the roof of the apartment blocks with camera and soundman looking for the best shot - no one was safe!

After a trip out I was dozing on a sun lounger when I became aware of a shadow covering my face. I opened my eyes to find Stephen hovering with his trusted two, armed with long, short and probably in-between lenses focusing on me. The big fluffy sound mike was in position. "Can we do an interview Sharron?" Someone had told them I was talkative!

"No." I didn't mean to be awkward but I felt intimidated. When I'm lying down, unable to move let alone sit up, I sometimes feel defenceless. I'm not a negative person by nature and I didn't want to be portrayed as a victim lying helpless. I have got used to people standing over me when I'm sitting up in the wheelchair but I can't bear more than one person standing over me even when I'm in my own surroundings - it is a source of contention. I feel closed in - trapped.

I made some crack about not getting my best side and having a bad hair day. They kindly rescheduled for the next morning. Stephen probably never realised as he sprawled on the floor (out of camera angle) how reversed the roles were from the day before. I was now positive, direct and sitting tall. I took every opportunity to plug my first book *Jump Jockeys* and we laughed and joked in between takes. My whole attitude changed by stature.

It was quite difficult for all the newcomers and the first year marker had hardly passed for Rebecca Hewitt, 32, and her husband Richard. Rebecca was a company secretary and had been placed a number of times in the North Western area point-to-points. Her paralysing fall came in a Hunter Chase at Hereford.

I'd met her once whilst she was recuperating in Oswestry Orthopaedic Hospital where I had also done time! She told me she had been standing down near the last hurdle when I had my fall. She and Richard had also ridden out for Alan Bailey who trained a horse owned by Richard's father, so we had a bit in common. That being said, we didn't chat about our predicament. Rebecca was still raw and Richard was obviously devastated. The last thing she needed was me in her face!

I remember how I had felt at times when words of encouragement would fall on deaf ears but her demure look struck me - she was a very attractive woman even in her sadness.

The year before, I'd met Barbara Towler, 34, and her husband, Andrew, who were both squadron leaders in the RAF. Barbara had been riding out for trainer John Upson and was preparing to ride in the Grand Military Gold Cup at Sandown. Her dream ended when she broke her back in a point-to-point on only her third ride, leaving her paralysed from the waist down. Now she was making the same journey as I had but she was much more fragile. A pretty petite blond who was consumed with anguish at how she'd been left and angered at the way she had been treated in hospital. She was a squadron leader who felt both mentally and physically violated.

"Shit happens Barb," Andrew had said in the early days. After nine years of marriage he became her stability when the light at the end of the tunnel was an oncoming train - he was her rock when she needed somewhere to lean on and man enough to face the adversity with her.

In Barbara and Rebecca the wounds ran deep and I hoped their anger would soon be replaced; had they not realised that this could happen? Or were they openly confronting the situation whilst I stayed behind my own bravado - always saying it was different for me. Why? I don't know, it just is - I was out there more. Thick and brash or just plain old black and white!

There were times when I felt envious: they were both so attractive

In 1982, I aimed to be champ.

PHOTOGRAPH COURTESY OF BARN OWL.

Leading the boys - room for improvement! (1985)

Me on the left jumping the last on 'Fourth Tudor' on my way to victory at Huntingdon (1988).

My first ride for Henry Cecil on 'Exceptional Bid', St Leger day (1990).
PHOTOGRAPH COURTESY OF KENNETH BRIGHT PHOTOGRAPHY.

Beating my great friend Lydia Pearce on 'Rose Glen', my last winner (1991).
PHOTOGRAPH COURTESY OF KENNETH BRIGHT PHOTOGRAPHY.

Mum and myself at Jump Jockeys *book launch (1996).*

All together for mum's sixtieth birthday. From left to right: Justine, Clive, Kelly, mum, Mark and myself.

My niece, Alyshia and nephews, Brodie (left) and Jake (right).

My nephews, James (left) and Matthew (right).

My last Sunday with the boys before returning home. From left to right: Trevor Rees-Jones, John Platt, myself, Brett Hollywell, Sean Arnold, Martin Ord and the late Arthur Jones (February 1992).

At a barbeque. From left to right: Glynn Jones, Johnny Rees, Frank Lodsdail, Brett Hollywell and Robin Chilton (1992).

Michael Caulfield (left), myself and Richard Phillips (1996).

At the House of Commons. Mr El Masry (front left), Lord Gowrie (back left), Richard Burridge (middle), Owen Paterson (right) and myself (December 1997).

Robin and Jan Chilton's wedding (1997).

Partying at the Sweeney Hall with John Platt (left) and Robin Chilton (right) (1999).

and petite - next to them I felt like a whale; when their husbands picked them up effortlessly out of their chairs and jumped in the pool with a laugh and a big splash; when they all swam unaided and free; when a wink or smile of reassurance is every word and more.

I wondered if it was easier to have someone to love you even when life throws one of its cruellest blows or was it easier to face the monstrosity alone - not having to deal with your lover's emotion - not having to worry that they may no longer find you appealing? A part of the whole scenario that I'd never had to address. What I don't have or can't do is dismissed out of hand but that doesn't mean I do not think about it.

Unfortunately Rebecca and Richard could not sustain their three-year marriage but a strong friendship has been borne out and to salvage something out of this kind of debacle is an achievement. Not everything can survive the card that is dealt.

So over the years many friendships have been made and for me in particular, Linda and Johnny O'Hara have become very special people in my life. Former jump jockey Johnny's career-ending fall came at Newcastle when his horse fell and another came crashing down on top of him. He eventually woke up to find he had broken both collar bones, ribs, nose, not to mention the spinal injuries (which would later curb his mobility as time passed); oh, and lost his teeth - all of them!

He can walk short distances slowly with Linda's help (giving me the opportunity to nickname him 'Lightning') and uses a scooter for getting around. As always in racing, there is a tale to tell. Unbeknown to me, Linda and Johnny were at Carlisle in November 1990 where I was riding in an Amateur Hurdle for trainer, Wilf Storey. Wilf asked me if I would like to ride schooling round the track for a lady permit holder after the last race. Keen as ever and without hesitation, I said yes. I would be accompanied by jockey Liam O'Hara, who was riding for another trainer and we would be covering about a mile and a half of the track, taking in the hurdles as they came.

I went into the paddock to be legged up on a somewhat agitated grey that I'd been assured jumped well - as it had been showjumping! The schooling session went all right but I recommended a few more before it ran. So when I first met Linda and Johnny he took great delight in telling me - and everyone else - about the time he stayed to watch his son schooling. In his strong Irish accent he recalled: "I remember seeing you at Carlisle when you had a ride for Wilf Storey. Bejesus, I said to Wilf - who's the bird you've got riding for you? If I'd have been ten years younger I'd have told Liam to get off that horse - you were a right little cracker!" I replied "Were?" and he came back with "Aah, bejesus, you still are" - and we've been friends ever since.

The holidays have become yet another reason for me to feel lucky. The sport I love so much - the sport in which I was maimed due to my own enthusiasm - has not treated me, or any other injured jockey, as a spent force. For ten days our disabilities fade into the background as we recall the races we won and have brilliant excuses for the ones that we lost!

Should any injured jockey need help the IJF hold out a lifeline and if at first it is rebuffed they don't take umbrage. They offer it again and again! In return we must be grateful for the unstinting work of the Injured Jockeys Fund whose Chief Executive, Jeremy Richardson, and daily administration staff operate from the headquarters of this marvellous organisation - not forgetting the ladies who process Christmas orders and pack thousands of parcels!

Then of course there are the many thousands of people who love going racing. They see the colour and the glamour - autograph hunters go home pleased because their favourite jockey has not only obliged with a signature but also ridden a winner. Many of them buy the Christmas cards, calendars and other goods that are on sale at racecourses throughout the country. They must also be applauded, for every pen or diary that is purchased means that a hero from yesteryear is receiving support after a bone-crushing and life threatening fall.

Statistics over the last three years show 1 fall per 220/250 rides - flat jockeys; 1 fall per 14/16 rides - jump jockeys. Since 1996 there have been 13 career ending injuries to jump jockeys; 3 for flat jockeys.

In 1999 Robert Hitchings, who owned many good horses, gave a wonderful gesture of a million pounds to the holiday fund in memory of his wife. The holidays are now guaranteed forever and quite rightly named The Robert and Elizabeth Hitchins Holiday. Sadly, Mr Hitchins passed away only a few weeks after our 2001 holiday where another three boys in need of a holiday joined us, Tim Sprake, Scott Taylor and Shane Broderick. I hope Mr Hitchens knew how much his gift was appreciated - I'm sure he did.

Heaven Passed By

Heaven passed me by
Hovered below the sun
Silently slipped through blue sky,
And the ground never smelt so green
Never felt so warm
In this pain-free dream.
I tried to reach out my hand
But wasn't allowed to touch
The forever golden sand,
It's not hard to forget to stay
Never felt so cold
On a hot summer's day.

I lay down my head - still there is a hero in my eyes
I lay down my heart - still the love never dies...

Heaven passed you by
Hovered in the afternoon air
Silently disappeared into black sky,
And the panicking rush
That never felt real
In the pain-free morning hush.
You tried to reach out so far
But weren't allowed to touch
The forever sparkling stars.
It's much harder to stay
Only the bravest can survive
On a cold winter's day.

Lay down your head - still the hero in our eyes
Lay down your heart - still the love never dies...

CHAPTER FIVE

MY MOTHER'S LOVE

How does somebody tell a mother that her young, vibrant daughter will never walk again; paralysed from the neck down, she will spend the rest of her days in a wheelchair?

And how is a mother supposed to react to this?

The desolation will forever torment my mother...

My mother has had her share of misery and, just to put the icing on the cake, I go and devastate her world a little bit more. Being abandoned with four children aged thirteen, ten, six and three in 1970 would have destroyed a weaker woman. A woman whose aim in life was quite simply to be a good mother and wife, bring up her children to the best of her ability with, of course, the love and support of a doting husband. Didn't happen.

My childhood was spent until 1972 living in Coley; a piece of countryside that lies on the borders of Halifax and Bradford. After that the cobbled back streets of Bradford became a familiar playing area. My determination to succeed in a profession that was a far cry from my roots or anything my family or friends could ever imagine made me selfish, self-centred and, at times, I put that burning ambition before loved ones. I was trying to make my mother proud of me by having the Murgatroyd name forever in the record books as being 'A Champion Lady Jockey'. I often dreamt about the day when it finally came, she would be there and all the pain and tears of the past would pale into insignificance - for a while anyway.

I was the only one of the family who didn't attend my youngest brother, Mark's, wedding. An unfortunate change of date with the wedding made it clash with an Amateur Race at Newmarket. Alan Bailey casually said, "Well, I'll get somebody else to ride if you don't want to". Sorry - but opportunities can be few and far between. I'd worked damned hard for every scrappy ride I could get. I had a choice. I could go to my brother's wedding and maybe watch my ride winning at Newmarket with another jockey or I could stay at home and ride it myself. Would I have been good company at the wedding or marred the most important day of my brother's life? Was I also secretly glad that I wouldn't have to see my mother having to go through yet another crushing family occasion alone because of her ex-husband?

She would also have loved to see at least one of her daughters walking down the aisle but one was too busy with horses and the other, my sister Justine, too busy riding her Harley Davidson - although she is now settled with her partner David. I used to joke with my mum saying, "Well, there will be no worries at my wedding with seating arrangements in the marquee!"

I know my mother would agree that our relationship has, sadly, deteriorated since my accident. I feel we are both at fault for this; for my part I am continually pushing her away and trying to prove that I can cope with my own life. I don't need sheltering or protecting, I'm a fully-grown woman in control - and take exception when she tends to treat me like a child. For her part, first and foremost, I am her child.

Our closeness, I feel, was borne out of my parents' marriage debris caused by his infidelity. For whatever reasons I was the only one who seemed to grasp the whole plot. My younger brother and sister were oblivious to the situation because of their age. My older brother, Clive, who idolised his father, was distraught and that wretchedness clouded his perception of my mother's pain. For many years he would flit between parents - every time he was thrown out of dad's house he'd turn up at mum's, always at some unearthly hour - suitcase in hand - he was never turned away. So that just left me savvy - all eyes and ears. Maybe this stemmed from one small but significant lie he told me; he could have said it to any of the others, but he told the wrong child...

The first few nights after he'd packed up and left, I would listen to her consoling Clive as he cried, asking when his dad was coming home or, as he heard a passing car and saw a flash of headlights, "Is that him now?" When she finally returned to her own room she would weep softly, ironically I would lie in bed almost paralysed not knowing what to do until sleep finally got the better of me. There were also many 'phone calls between my parents to see if there was any way back to the comfortable lifestyle we had all been living - the bedroom 'phone extension came in very handy for me.

By the time I was twelve we had lived with my granddad for four months and then we moved to Rowentree Drive (the posh end of a council estate). My mother had her work cut out there with two jobs but we never went hungry - she often did. Even though we still saw our dad from time to time (and one year had a week in Cornwall) it was always awkward for me. I can understand that he may not have loved my mum anymore but the lie that his behaviour "was all in her mind" was unforgivable. Even though I had done what most adolescent girls would (I took my anger at my mum's pain out on him at every opportunity), as a father shouldn't he have realised this?

I know it must have seemed to him that we only ever wanted money for a new coat or some other item but what else could he give us - not love - not support. He never said "you are my children, I love you dearly" - I'm sure I would have remembered that! So it probably wasn't such of a surprise when three times between the ages of fourteen and sixteen, (during my mother's second, even more horrendous and abusive marriage), I asked for his help - three times I was turned away and from then on he just became irrelevant in my life.

A half-hearted attempt for him and I to reconcile after my accident failed. He couldn't handle my abruptness or my 'yes' and 'no' answers when he telephoned me in the first months on my return home (unlike my mother). I also didn't have an ounce of respect for him, but at least he had been some help for my mother. He'd brought her to see me mid-week and bunged her a few quid while I was in hospital and I basically used him for as long as we needed to.

As soon as I was sixteen, after months of indecision about a career and an irate 'Jekyll and Hyde' stepfather calling me lazy and saying I didn't want to work, I rejoiced in securing a job for racehorse trainer Bob Ward. Now it was my turn to abandon my younger brother and sister, who I had helped to look after for those tumultuous years, and my mother. She had given me everything that was within her capabilities. Without a second thought I boarded a train bound for Doncaster. My mum cried for a week or more not solely because she was distressed at only being able to give me five pounds.

My mother, brother and sister would endure two and a half more years of rows, fighting and despicable behaviour before my mother secured herself a council flat. It must have been demoralising for her to realise that this man whom she had married and who, on the surface (and in company) was a charming person, commended for promising to give her and her children love and security - would turn out to be so horrendous.

It was February 1979 and the snow fell thickly when I drove from Gisburn in Lancashire (where I had moved to work for Tony Dickinson) back to Shipley to help my mother load up her belongings and get out of a five-year marriage - where the badness far outweighed the good.

She has been alone since then - well almost. The workload has stayed with her. I used to go home for the odd weekend and flake out on the settee after a delicious meal. My mother understandably used to make a bit of a fuss because she didn't see me so often. This was much to the annoyance of Mark and Justine who, except for my mother's unconditional love, could still have been hiding in the cupboard under the stairs with only a candle for the comfort of light - the atmosphere was either brewing or settling after yet another 'Hyde' performance. I have found out a lot about their closeness and perception of me lately. Apparently I didn't endear myself to them as I would 'swan in and out without a good word to say', whilst they were going through the usual phases of growing up.

It was 1984 when my mother was granted custody and guardianship of my niece Kelly (Clive's daughter) after her mother Jackie tragically died from a brain tumour a year earlier at the age of 25. Jackie's parents naturally thought they should have Kelly but my mother never wavered over bringing up her grandchild even though she had reached a stage when her life could have become easier. My mum had been a mainstay in Kelly's life from the day she was born. So it was right and fitting that the three-year-old child who had lived at first in my mum's flat and then next door (with her mother) ever since, should remain with her paternal grandmother with father on hand.

By this time Mark had already met his intended, Helen, whose mother has been friends with my mum since their school days. They were marvellous with Kelly as was Justine, but obviously I again wasn't around that often. Not until I threw all their lives into disarray. Mum and Kelly had always enjoyed a short summer break in Newmarket but that year would see many changes for us all - breaking my mother's heart just a little bit more…

While I had to endure seven weeks in head callipers at Oswestry my mum stayed too. Kelly, then aged 12, went to live with her dad and his wife of only a few months, Bonita. At least my mother (who didn't know whether she was coming or going) wouldn't have to worry about Kelly - she was in safe hands; but she would never return to live with her grandma.

It was quite often a hellish journey for my family to travel from Yorkshire to the market town of Oswestry. Clive and Mark were working for my dad at that time so it was easier to get off work early. Even though they had busy lives of their own, they all visited regularly and I am so sorry that I brought this encumbrance into the lives of my brothers, Clive and Mark, their families and my sister Justine - yet so glad it was me and not one of them.

I could have had my spill anywhere - luckily for me I was only a few miles away from my riding colleague Diana Jones and her family. They gave my mother and me selfless support. Justine even spent a whole week of her holiday staying at the Jones' so she could visit me every day in hospital: "I never thought I would be peeling grapes for you to eat" - we both laughed. Justine and I never had a close sister relationship. I was the older sister she felt she never had - subsequently we have often clashed and although we are very different there is a kindred spirit between us and we can always reveal our feelings in verse.

On the 13th day of August in 1991, eleven days after my fall, she did just that:

Who do I cry for?

Who do I cry for?
Is it for you or for me?
Oh Sister all we wanted was to be free,
So we put on a brave face as we look at you
Holding on to your hand and holding on to you.
We'll never let you go or leave you alone
Our hearts your roots is our home.

I say my prayers for you each night
But you must promise never to give up this fight.
God knows so many people care
And if they could your pain they would share.
Even if the future does look black
Be brave for me don't let that courage crack,
There's so much time ahead of us yet
And there's so much hope don't ever forget.

So if on that racecourse your spirit lies
And you feel without it a part of you dies.
Just think of all the glory you've touched and seen
On moors of heather and pastures green.
But I know deep down in my heart
That this is not the end it's just the start,
There'll be many more winning posts you'll fly on by
And then there will be happiness where my tears now lie.

So who do I cry for
Is it for me or for you?
Oh sister what does this life put us through
But it's all just another hurdle,
Another wave crashing on the beach
And it's all here for us and it's all in our reach
So never let me go or leave me alone
Our hearts my roots is our home.

My undisputed decision to return home to Becklyn in Newmarket - where I had travelled from on the fateful day - has always felt right. So now my mum and family come and stay as often as they can. My mum comes for Christmas with Justine and David or my niece Kelly and fiancé Barry Turner. Mark, wife Helen and my nephews Matthew and James have celebrated quite a few New Years with us as well as summer holidays. Eldest brother Clive, wife Bonita with niece Alyshia and twin nephews Brodie and Jake also come to stay in the summertime.

During the summer, mainly when Nancy has her holiday, mum comes down for a few weeks on her own leaving the flat she is deeply proud of and which she calls her 'Little Blue Haven'. Now she is known down here as 'Thelmareachforthebleachatthelittlebluehaven.com'. She has become even more fastidious about the cleanliness of dishcloths and tea towels than ever before and although the girls and I tell her to take it easy, she goes round like a whirling dervish looking for jobs to do!

On one of these cleaning excursions in my kitchen she found a tupperware container in the back of a cupboard. I heard her asking Janet what it was - she didn't know. Then my mum said it looked like herbs or something, but it stank! A few months earlier I had acquired this 'herbal remedy' to put in tea or coffee - to alleviate any neck or shoulder pain - best left to brew in a teapot. My mum heard me asking one of the girls if she had found me a one-person teapot, and no was the answer to that. On her next visit she duly turned up with a gift, one small white teapot with a blue flower. By then I had one of my own which just happened to be all blue. The herbal remedy had not worked at all no matter how much I used or brewed! It had been pushed to the back of the cupboard. My cups of tea tasted better straight from the cup after all I told my mum. "Can I have your blue teapot for my flat then?" "Of course you can mum." And the 'herbal remedy?' She told me to sling it - it stank!

No job is too big or too small and she loves entertaining, be it a lunch or dinner party. Her baking is now renowned in this part of the world and dozens of buns and cakes of different varieties are magically produced from my kitchen and eaten or parcelled up for the workers, visitors and children, who receive special smaller ones!

My apparent lack of appreciation upset her deeply after she had yet again bent over backwards to ensure that my fortieth birthday, (which lasted a whole weekend) was superb. I know it's not too late to be grateful.

There are never parties or barbecues that go by without an Oswestry presence. I met the rugby boys through the Jones' and we've been friends ever since. But those rugby boys are on a yellow card and soon off to the sin bin! They could be banned because they get me into terrible trouble with my mum for drinking too much. "Thelma," they say, "She'll be alright, she's one of the boys - and no she won't fall out of the chair - not until we spin her a bit faster!" In the morning she insists on the table being laid for breakfast (forever the perfectionist); all guests must be fed before they leave. Then she has to go home for a rest!

One of the things my mum told me was, "Grab your happiness while you can, because you never know how long it will last." Well I did that alright, but in hindsight (the wonderful hindsight) I could have grabbed a few handfuls more. I don't make that mistake now, although it's curbed somewhat! A recent family rift has seen my mother's love stretched to the limits where she had to be both conciliatory and diplomatic and it makes me wonder how or when she grabs any happiness for herself.

So my mother is a very special lady who has played a pivotal role in all our lives and should be highly praised on her achievement in keeping her children safe and above all loved... Now she can be secure in the knowledge that we, her children and Kelly (now 22), without living in each other's pockets or always 'seeing eye to eye', at the end of the day are and always will be there for each other. That she can be assured of - and we are all guilty of not fully appreciating her.

Her only fault is caring, worrying and loving her now adult children and grandchildren too much.

Not such a bad fault, I feel...

Thanking You

Thank you - for the life
We have found.
Thank you - for the strength
Deep within.
Thank you - our Mother
For you have kept us from giving in.

And we don't even realise,
With the harsh words we speak
How we hurt you so.
Oh sweet Mother of ours,
You with never a word unkind
Stand there by our side,
Waiting for us to turn
Someone there to find.

Thank you - for being
Our friend.
Thank you - for the care
And all the loving.
Thank you - for a hand to hold
When we feel alone.

With arms ever stretching out
Stretching out for us.
Our Mother
Our guiding light;
Your words of encouragement
We can hear in the long
And lonely night.
Run dry now any tears we have wept
We are forever in your debt.

OUR LOVE ALWAYS
CLIVE, SHARRON, MARK, JUSTINE
& KELLY

CHAPTER SIX

NIL DESPERANDUM

After the reception of *Jump Jockeys Don't Cry,* Peter Rossdale and Ian McIntyre thought it would be a good idea if I wrote a book of my poetry. There had been many positive remarks about the poems that had been featured in the book. What I didn't realise was that in their minds it would be published that very same year. By this time it was nearly the end of May '97! "How many poems have you got?" Ian enquired. "How many do you want?"

I only had about five hundred million! Starting from the age of 13.

My next task was to read through my old handwritten poem book, adorned by a now-scuffed picture of David Bowie. This brought back memories that would never have been referred to if I'd still been riding. Having discussed the layout and time span of the pending work I selected ones that I thought were relevant. My poems read like a diary of my life, the first entry was 1973 and as I turned each page I instantly knew where, when and about whom I had written them.

I knew which of them were true - and which were pure fantasy. I came face to face with some of the darkest days of my adolescence (which had become worse when we moved from Yeadon to Saltaire in early '76) when all I wanted to do was escape from the real world. The outside influences of the time were heavily portrayed and some were not for interpretation - some were subversive (only I would ever know what I meant if anyone happened to read them). I picked through these carefully, there were some that I could explain to Ian - but others would stay forever enclosed between the ageing pages, deeply private. It would be embarrassing not only for their sexual connotations but also mostly because the earlier ones were speculation and not about real life.

Then there were the ones that captured reality - but I still felt it was too soon (hello dumbo, you are ... 37) to reveal in front of my mother and Ian details of how I had become so familiar with soft drugs at the age of 14. How I would be forever grateful to one guy who stopped me trying anything too hard like LSD... and that's not pounds shillings and pence!

The laborious task started. First of all I selected which poems I thought were relevant and then I had to type them all into my computer, easier said than done! I had to structure my day around my twice-weekly physio visits: work for a couple of hours, take a break - and then recommence typing for another couple of hours. This brought me up to 4pm when I would go into the lounge and read the papers - the only two hours in a day when I was left completely alone.

I was feeling really well and happy with the direction my life was taking. Until a telephone call from Paula Bloomfield (who is married to my friend Peter) with the dreadful news that our former head lad at Alan Bailey's and Alan's almost life-time friend, Fred Town, had been killed as he was cycling to work. This soon stopped me feeling happy about anything. He was a dear man. Fred had been hit by a van on the Cambridge road just by the Golf Links. His daughter Melody had only the week before dropped in an invitation for his surprise 60th birthday party. It had taken a long time for Fred to get used to my new situation after being one of my greatest supporters. Now instead of attending his birthday party - we would be at his funeral. It was a very sad time...

It was around this time that I also received a letter from a man who used to be in racing but was now living in London. He had written to me after reading *Jump Jockeys* and said that it had helped him in his own 'fight against illness' - as a recovering alcoholic. He asked if I would write a poem for him and I telephoned to explain it was quite hard to write about somebody I didn't know. In a way I was trying to put him off as I didn't want a repetition of what had happened in hospital (on more than one occasion) whereby complete strangers began to write and visit me with worrying regularity. I explained I would try and left it at that. This played on my mind and, by the Monday, I relayed the request to Joan and enquired what could I write about an alcoholic in rehabilitation? A subject I knew nothing about. Joan gave me two words - Nil Desperandum. Now most people know I didn't attend school very often; I do know a couple of words in French but Latin 'nil point' - I asked Joan " What does that mean then?" "Never despair."

Thank you, Joan - you've just given me the title for his poem. That day I wrote *Nil Desperandum* and sent it to him. On the day he received it he telephoned to say thank you, he'd taken it to show others at his Rehabilitation Unit and asked me if I would go in to give a talk. I replied that if he arranged it I would, pleased that I'd been able to help him - even after he added it was to be held in the psychiatric ward (we're not all nutters) - but he never came back to me on that.

My Thursday sessions at the horse and trap fitted in well at first but my initial enthusiasm had started to wane. I had been writing for a couple of hours in the morning and resuming for an hour in the afternoon. This was fine to begin with, but the imminent changeover at the stables, the winding down of driving competitions (the main reason for being there) and alteration to a Wednesday gave me no choice but to dedicate my time to finishing this next book. The experience had been wonderful and I would recommend the sport to anyone who had the opportunity. However, even though I had been joyful when I felt that first tug of the reins on my wrists from the horse's mouth, I found my thirst for a racing-orientated replacement had gone. Working under the pressure of a deadline gave me a real buzz - I had a job to do even on the days I felt unwell.

It was June and I had a long way to go.

I was pleased with my efforts when Ian McIntyre visited to look at my first 20 poems. I can still see him now perusing my 'raw for my eyes only material' with a bemused look on his face. Ian discarded some of my precious work and, for a moment, I felt deflated until he commented that yes, he thought I had something - he didn't really know what - but when they were whipped up into coherent verse with proper stanzas (didn't see that one coming) then they would become readable. The bad use of commas and semi-colons - when used at all - jumped out so much a blind man could see them!

My long days with Ian were quite physically and mentally draining. He would point out what certain poems needed by way of balance and use of grammar. He would flick through saying "No good, no good, no good," and I would ask "Why?" He would then ask me to convince him. I would explain the meaning behind the poem; occasionally I'd win, persuading him to keep it in - and other times he'd win and I knew it would have to go! He was intrigued to know how old I was when I wrote some of the deep and varied poems; lines including 'Society of Man' spring to mind. After some of our meetings I would have to redo by word and verse, coming back time and time again until it was correct.

"And of course you will have to think of a title," Ian casually said as he packed his briefcase one evening.

"How about Nil Desperandum?" He smiled at that. Job done!

Two weeks into August and the strain began to tell. I was so annoyed with myself - why couldn't I type more and do longer hours? I felt tired and an oncoming bladder infection slowed me down even more. By now Ian and I were meeting three times a week, often the days would be from 1 in the afternoon until 6 pm. My mother came down, as some of the girls were taking holidays, and after typing in the morning I would go into the recliner where at least I could rest my body. I ached around my neck and shoulders whilst my legs throbbed with the all too familiar burning sensation; still Ian and I worked on. My mother and Ian would be passing the poems back and forth as discussion and alterations were made. My mother took the brunt of my frustration as it was all clear to me which of the poems I had amended and in what order they should appear. Despite the pressure she coped admirably, as always.

I had sensed an atmosphere between Michelle and myself but chose to ignore this, hoping it would soon rectify. At that time she worked on a Wednesday, Friday and every third weekend. My diet was the first stage of disagreement. She would suggest I eat some fruit or muesli for breakfast but I had never eaten at breakfast time and wasn't going to start now. All around my hairline, scurf began to build up even after washing my hair with every product available in Newmarket and the surrounding areas. One Monday morning when Joan had got me settled by the sun-filled window to read the papers, whilst she started with cleaning the bathroom - I felt a small tickle on the left-hand side of my forehead. When I gently rubbed it with the back of my hand I could not believe the big white flakes of skin that fell onto the paper. I called Joan and the only way to get rid of it was to literally scrub it off with a dry towel for about fifteen minutes. It was dreadful and the same procedure had to be done before I went to bed.

This was just the cusp of things to come.

I was busy writing and also there was my barbecue to plan and organise; I'd already booked an Elvis impersonator the previous May. I wanted the barbecue to take place on Saturday 2nd August but he was booked up until Saturday 31st so I settled for that. This turned out to be better for the rugby boys as it did not clash with Oswestry Annual Show. For me this event had even more significance because the previous year I cancelled it as my two closest friends Ali and Joss were both ill in hospital.

Ian and I had a very positive meeting on the Friday; we were on schedule, I just had to keep the work rate up for the next few weeks. He wanted all the poems finished before he took a break in Spain and then John Fuller, who was doing illustrations for some of the poems, could finish off his work. We had discussed the front and back cover of the book and as usual I gave my opinion! Ian had recruited Richard Snowball (who he knew and had worked with before) to design the cover. So it was all coming together. Ian told me to enjoy my barbecue and take a couple of days off - I deserved it - yes - on both counts.

My rift with Michelle had eased as she had told me of her own unhappiness within her marriage. I knew all too well about that vile emotional pain. Thank goodness I would never have to face that again. She must have had to drag herself out of bed on those days she was working, coming to get me up, showered and dressed. All her suggestions for my invaded constipated body were dismissed without a second thought. It was probably just a side effect from the antibiotics I told her. I knew what was best for me!

I was looking forward to seeing all my friends at the barbecue. It was unfortunate due to work or holiday, only Robin Chilton, girlfriend Jan

Adams and John Platt (Platty) could make the journey from Oswestry but Trev Rees-Jones, who had been working away for well over two years, was travelling up from London. Trev had told Robin not to get hammered until he had picked him up from Newmarket train station! The last time he had made the same trip was for my birthday in '95 so we had a lot of catching up to do. Robin had kept me informed about all the rugby boys (as he did them about me) and Trev was looking forward to the weekend bash. I knew it would be fun and crazy and I needed to let off steam. Big time!

When they arrived, Robin left Jan and Platty to unload the car of overnight bags and, most importantly, the beers whilst he told me that Trev's plans had been changed so he wouldn't be coming. "That's a shame he'll miss Elvis" but the beers were open by then and the partying had started.

Elvis, although only about five foot two, was brilliant. His white outfit was changed to black for his second entrance of the evening and we all had a good laugh when he spotted Petra leaving and began to chase her down the drive - it later came to light that many of the neighbours sat out and enjoyed listening to him. Midnight was an early time for us to come back inside but there was certainly a nip in the air. Robin and Platty had tipped a dustbin of iced water, that had been used to keep the drinks cold, over my niece Kelly and her friend, the Murgatroyd cheek alive and well but now very wet! My childhood friend Anne and her son Scott had made the journey from Yorkshire and had helped to put up a string of lantern lights as I told Scott at these do's everybody has to muck in - not to be confused with - mucking out! Although Andy wouldn't agree, especially on 'Hangover Sunday'.

After I'd been tucked up comfortably in bed, they all congregated in my bedroom but instead of the usual singing, we chatted and the high spirits continued whilst Mum sorted out some blankets for the floor sleepers! I know it was about 2.30am (as I'd flicked through the movie channel just in case sleep was not forthcoming) before we all settled down; unaware of the dramatic events that were unfolding involving our absent friend Trev...

We woke up to the awful news of the Paris car crash that shook the nation with the death of the Princess. The frivolity of the previous night had been replaced with a subdued atmosphere as bags were packed and goodbyes were brief - we were oblivious to the fact that Trev was involved and in the car at the time of the accident.

By early evening I was back in my recliner, more to relax from the exertions of the night before than through necessity. The news seemed to be on constantly (although it wasn't) and as I half dozed the broadcaster revealed the name of the only survivor. My body went into spasm, appearing to jump with total shock. I opened my eyes to see that Trev's smiling face appeared to fill the television screen. My mother placed her hand on my arm as if to restrain me but we remained silent.

I found myself caught up in a bizarre chain of events. By Monday the racing and tabloid press were ringing for details of our friendship. I was stunned to hear that they knew he was supposed to be at my barbecue. I felt safe with the racing journalists (as I had spoken to them on many occasions throughout my career and accident) but although I explained he was one of many rugby boys who visited me after my fall, they were not interested in anybody else.

I was particularly annoyed when a woman from the tabloid press rang with questions such as "What part did I play in his life?" and "Is it true you are a lady jockey?" I told her in no uncertain terms that she should get her facts right. She was obviously unaware of my situation. Yet again I was telephoned by the same paper and advised by a reporter that a 'no comment' could still be built into a story with sections used from the racing papers. When that particular article appeared I felt I had betrayed my friend.

I was in constant contact with Robin as many conflicting stories emerged and, as I strove to resume working on my book, my mind wandered easily and I frequently wrote to Trev with whom I felt empathy. It was the least I could do.

The rest of the month passed with suppressed emotion even though it wasn't my place to feel this way, I thought. My knotted up body and general well being were still worrying Michelle and she told Joan of her anxiety. "There is nothing wrong with me apart from this infection!" I protested. I wasn't going to change my lifestyle now. Head down, I ploughed on disregarding their concerns. I finished all the poems and handed them in to the publishers. Ian flew off to Spain leaving a contact number and then the doctor was called in to sort me out!

Within weeks I was back to as near normal as I can get! I had one small problem but with Lisa's efficiency and my determination a new poem that I'd just written and wanted incorporated in the book was faxed to Ian for his approval. I was pleased it could be included and Trev was home too.

One important lesson had been learnt during those last strenuous months. One day towards the end of the summer Michelle commented that I seemed more motivated! More motivated! I'd been working my butt off all summer - where had she been? It so easily could have blown up with either one of us telling the other to 'stuff it', but thankfully we didn't. With a bit of patience and realising the separate but emotional life we inadvertently found ourselves living, Michelle and I worked through our differences.

A few weeks later she told me that she'd read in a magazine that all the scurfy hairline was caused by stress and in my own paper I had read an article that proclaimed emotional turmoil can play havoc with your insides. We'd had a rough few months but we were back on track and now she can't wait to come to work!

On the 21st October '97 I started writing the poetic text of my third work, a colourfully illustrated book for children. The artwork was to be done by Newmarket's resident artist Jacquie Jones, who unbeknown to Ian McIntyre was an old colleague of mine (we first met in 1978), so we were both pleased to be working on this very different project. Ian had initially requested the book with a finishing date for the end of February; "Ahh, help!" As there is a lull in between finishing a book and its date of publication, I thought I'd crack on with the new one, pinch a few lengths at the gate! I knew I'd have to take time out to promote *Nil Desperandum* by doing the usual radio shows and press interviews I had experienced before. I started penning my next project with great enthusiasm. I recalled my childhood days when ponies ruled my friend Anne's and my own young life - marvelling at the flood of ideas that were coming easily.

Then everything seemed to start happening all at once but luckily I was now in good health after the stress of the summer months. Unfortunately the stress had not caused weight loss and although none of the girls had passed any comment of me gaining weight - I knew I was heavy. A visit to the hospital confirmed I was right, all 10st of me...

My own diet started and I knew I would have to be ruthless with myself and the daily intake of wine!

Mr El Masry (consultant orthopaedic surgeon at Oswestry hospital) had asked me to be one of the fund-raising patrons for the Midland Spinal Unit Appeal. Of course, I was delighted, immediately telling him of my recently finished book and that all proceeds from *Nil Desperandum* would go to this cause. My association with Oswestry was becoming ever stronger and this was yet another reason for me to visit more frequently. The two spinal wards were in dire need of refurbishment. There were many improvements to be made at an estimated cost of £3.5 million. After the initial London meeting, together with the rest of the committee members which included Lady Masham, Lord Gowrie, Rupert Moon (rugby player), Dennis Amiss MBE (cricketer) and Major John Warburton-Lee, a date was set when the launch would take place.

The launch would take place at the House Of Commons in December.

First and foremost though in my mind, was the marriage of my great now ex-rugby playing friend, Robin, to Jan which took place at the Sweeney Hall Hotel near Oswestry on 22nd November. I was particularly touched as they had individually asked me to write a poem.

Jan's was based on friends coming together and Robin wanted to tell Jan of his love. I nearly messed it all up by faxing the wrong verse to Jan, but luckily I realised in time. This was an important event for all of us and as it would be one of the first gatherings to include Trev since his accident - it would be emotional.

His appearance shocked me, this once tall, strong, handsome man bore little resemblance to the friend I knew - if I had passed him in the street, I wouldn't have recognised him. I was unprepared (despite our earlier telephone conversations) not for the massive facial injuries he had incurred but for his dramatic weight loss and the once thick, curly, blondish hair that had been reduced to a straight, thin, brown covering.

The wedding and reception were wonderful and I finally met Lara Burton. We'd both heard a lot about each other, sharing the same friends but at different times. She had started her physio course at Oswestry as I was leaving to come home. Lara volunteered with Alex Jones to look after me for the duration of the day and evening, so Janet could go off and have some time to herself. We all agreed we would have to pace ourselves with the alcohol intake - getting along straight away! The evening party was typically raucous and took over the whole hotel. It was around 4am when our own invitation to Robin and Jan's honeymoon suite was met with the firmest refusal Robin has ever given - even I couldn't persuade him to make us all coffee - "Not on this night!"

I arrived home tired not only because of the late night but I had witnessed and experienced many deep emotions over the weekend and took a few days to fully recover. So when a delay somewhere along the line meant it would be November 29th before *Nil Desperandum* was launched at the Bedford Lodge Hotel I wasn't too disappointed and this time it was much more low key. I wrote a poem instead of a speech, it was called 'Moments of Joy' and I had copies on different coloured paper laid out, asking for a contribution towards the spinal fund in return for a copy of the poem. This raised around £150 on the night which was a start for the appeal. As we were about to leave, the late arrival of friends Martin Norman (who used to deliver hay and straw to the Newmarket racing stables), his step mother Liz and her daughter, gave me no alternative but to have another late night!

Together with Jennie and Bruce Raymond, my mum and Janet, we stayed until all the paid-for wine had run out. Martin was pleased (after profusely apologising) that they were late and so was I - another piece of time to savour…

The 'Spiney' Appeal launch was in one of the function rooms at the House of Commons on Tuesday 2nd December. Peter Rossdale, Ian Wallace along with, from racing, Lord Oaksey and Michael Caulfield, attended showing their support for me and the project. Together with others, Mr El Masry had asked if I would make a speech in front of the many distinguished guests. I readily agreed, as always - then realised what it entailed and needed a drink! However, on the day I was unfazed; there was a job to do and it was imperative that I did it properly. For the good of the cause.

My House of Commons speech went like this:

Good afternoon ladies and gentlemen.

I was delighted when asked to be a fund raising patron for the Midland Spinal Unit, knowing only too well the desperate need for refurbishment and my stay was over six years ago.

Nearly every day of Mr El Masry's life he has to tell somebody's mother and father, husband or wife, son or daughter, that one of their loved ones has suffered a spinal cord injury and will spend the rest of their life in a wheelchair.

His life's work and knowledge makes not one iota of difference to this particular part of his job. He has not become inured to this task, he says these words with care and understanding.

One of the main problems of the unit is the demoralising lack of privacy at a time of both physical and emotional trauma. And dealing with this, no matter how tough we think we are, is not helped by being in a mixed ward with only thin curtains and insufficient space between beds. For a time I was the only woman amongst 15 men and, despite having worked in a male orientated world, I still found this unpleasant.

Although there is some need to nurse spinal injuries together for moral support, dignity is paramount, there are women and men - for all I know - whose rehabilitation has been psychologically hindered. This is not good enough!

It is not good enough that a storeroom doubles up as a resuscitation room.

It is not good enough that the ward layout is still in the style of the 1920s.

It is not good enough that oxygen is provided by an old fashioned cylinder by the bed.

And

It is not good enough that there is not even wheelchair access throughout.

I will be forever grateful for the treatment and care I received during my stay at Oswestry. They pointed me in the right direction, by instilling in me that I still had a lot to offer in life. I am still the same person and can still be in control albeit with constant help. The first time Mr El Masry told me that life doesn't stop just because you are in a wheelchair, I didn't believe him - I do now.

So maybe with your help other people will reap the benefit as we bring Mr El Masry's spinal unit into the 21st century.

Thank you…

I was certainly getting about. "Have wheelchair will travel," I told Richard Phillips when he rang enquiring as to my whereabouts on three or four occasions when he'd only been able to speak to my answerphone. Laughing, he retorted, " You get where water can't." The time had come for a date to be fixed for my annual Yuletide lunch. The first took place in '93. Richard and Gee Armytage were going to take me out but my mum said she would cook the lunch. It started with four people and ended up being eight!

It has become a firm fixture where the order of the day starts with Bellini's. This is a concoction of champagne, peach schnapps and a dash of orange juice but they are only drunk if Richard turns up with inferior bubbly. He doesn't now but (when I told him about writing this book, his words were "Tell it as it is," so I am and) he did!

A different set of guests have been invited each year to join the three of us and I sometimes make up a question and answer quiz. We have only missed one and that was the year we lost Ali Thom.

In the New Year of '98 it was back to work on *Pony Days* which would be my third book in as many years. It wouldn't write itself so I knuckled down looking for inspiration but it wasn't flowing like it had before Christmas. One day (when I definitely needed the blinkers on) I came up with an idea to raise money for the appeal fund. I don't know why I hadn't thought of it sooner. 'A Sponsored Wheelchair Push'. "Oh yeah?" said the voice in my head - "From where to where?" Lands End to John O'Groats. No, I mean the other way round. Ian Botham walked it - I with a load of pushers could be pushed it!

I wrote to Mr Botham sending him a *Jump Jockeys* book free, of course. His publicist sent back some bumph with a map of the route he took. It had the mileage - 912 miles in 35 days - averaging 28 miles a day. The least amount of miles in a day was 19, the most 37. Now my maths isn't very good but even I could work out that it was 426 miles before you got out of Scotland! I decided against it - anyway, I didn't want to upstage him.

Instead I opted for a much more achievable task.

My initial correspondence with Major Webster, Clerk of Bangor racecourse, was in January. I told him my outline plan for a wheelchair push retracing my journey on the day of my fall, from the last hurdle at Bangor to Wrexham Casualty and then onto the Orthopaedic Hospital in Oswestry. He thought it was a good idea. We started the ball rolling, even though the event wasn't taking place until Friday 31st July. There was a lot of organising to do. I had to find jockeys, past, present or future, to push me, map out a route and draft a letter for sponsorship. I had also been approached to do a television documentary. No rest for the wicked I fear!

The scheduled date of the finished text for *Pony Days* by the end of February went awry. After a good start I came to a shuddering halt. I needed some fresh inspiration but it just wasn't there. It was a relief when Ian rang to say he wouldn't need the completed text until the end of March. The graphic designer man would not be able to start until then. I told him I was struggling but apparently that is common and if I tried to force things, neither of us would be satisfied with the end product!

The impending television documentary, which had been arranged by Jean Goodman, was going to take nearly two weeks to film. Jean is a well-known author and had written an article about me, for a local paper. She had been an associate of Ian's at one time and played an instrumental role by liaising with the film director. The 'lights, camera, action' was due to begin during the first couple of weeks in February. Ian suggested I took the opportunity to freshen up; a short sabbatical from writing, so everything was working in house.

The director, Clive Dunn, soundman, Robin Shaw, and cameraman, Geoff Lloyd, arrived on 10th February and for the next ten days you would have thought we were doing some epic film instead of a half hour fly-on-the wall documentary. There were three fundamental points that Clive wanted to convey apart from my day to day routine: my social life, charity work and riding 'Fiefdom'.

I'd been aboard my now semi-retired former racehorse once since my body had been paralysed but that was just in his stable. It had been brilliant then and it would be even better this time, I told Andy Young who would be in the saddle as well as holding me in position. "Why is that then?" he enquired. "Because, Andy mate, we are going out into the lunge ring - I'm ready to start riding out again!" His army training came in handy as he planned and prepared for the big day.

When I spoke to Clive about the running order of events, I also told him about my appeal fund meeting with Mr El Masry. He was keen to get that on film and asked me what I felt about returning to Bangor (if it was feasible with his budget). I had already been back to the racecourse I told him - it was the first outing I had when I was still in rehabilitation at Oswestry. I had not been emotional - just very pleased to be back in the real world.

So it held no fears. Yes - I was up for a bit of filming at Bangor!

We all had a lot of fun during the filming and the saying of the day became 'can you just do that again…' The girls and I took it in our stride and the only disappointing thing was that we were funnier off camera than on! The crew enjoyed their day filming at Huntingdon races, the people they met and interviewed. By the end they understood why I wasn't bitter. They had tried to get me to say how unhappy I was to have had my life destroyed by this cruel turn of fate. I disagreed; yes my life had changed but it's not, by any means, destroyed. "If it were, you wouldn't be here now, laughing at my jokes, would you?" I've ridden against and with some of the best lady jockeys in Europe and most definitely the best jump jockeys in the world. Not to mention my couple of spins in the Dickins Invitation Pro/Am races, where my name figured on the runners and riders board next to Pat Eddery, one of the greatest flat jockeys of the present day. I have a supportive family, closer friends now than before and feel privileged to have experienced the great camaraderie I shared with my lady and male riding colleagues in the 80s.

The following Friday (after a weekend in Oswestry) the crew filmed the last part of the documentary showing me riding my ex-racehorse 'Fiefdom' who was 18 years old then. He was still a bit bargy but seemed to know he had to stand still whilst I was hoiked up onto his back. Andy, then got on behind me and held me in position whilst steering 'Fiefdom' at the same time. It was a beautiful sunny day for February and a poignant but fulfilling moment - we rode round the lunge ring - and we even had a trot - but I couldn't persuade Andy to kick him on into a canter. The feeling was better than before - but I knew that would be as good as it gets…

The documentary was called 'The Last Fling', narrated by actress Amanda Burton. I wanted Bryan Adams singing 'Everything I Do (I Do For You)' at the end as I rode 'Fiefdom' but the BBC East programme makers' budget could not run to that! I was more than happy for the disabled children of 'Chicken Shed' to sing their song and it was much more apt.

My appearance in the documentary saddened me. I looked bloated in the face and even fatter in the body. I had been dieting strictly and had cut the wine to two small glasses at night except when I went out. But I was determined to carry on.

The break from writing did me good and by the time my holiday with the Injured Jockeys Fund in April came round, which was much needed and appreciated, I only had to write the introduction to my third book *Pony Days* which I titled 'Horses Wonderful Horses'.

Over the next two months I represented the Injured Jockeys Fund at

Newmarket Bowls Club where their fund raising match made a record £1,500. I enjoy doing speeches at events where many people follow racing and are genuinely interested in what happens to jockeys who have injuries. I came home with several bottles of spirits kindly given to me by the raffle ticket winners.

It was great to be invited to the Timeform Dinner at York - this annual event raises phenomenal amounts of money for various charities the main recipient being Macmillan Cancer Relief Fund. Timeform is an international company that produces information on every racehorse currently racing in Britain including details of the performances of top class horses racing abroad. Jim McGrath, the managing director of the company as well as a Channel Four racing presenter, must have been checking my form and noticed I had ridden in the first running of the Queen Mother's Cup 10 years previously. His conscience obviously pricked - hence the invitation, and he also insisted that my mother be present. Unbeknown to me Reg Griffin, the Chairman of the company, wanted me to receive a Timeform Special Award, apparently there were two main runners - the recently retired Mark Dwyer and myself (sorry, Mark - but you did win a Gold Cup!). It was very special for me because I was being recognised by a worldwide racing organisation.

I was also very kindly invited to an insurance company's regional hospitality dinner with Richard Phillips and Gee Armytage after racing at Newmarket. One of the managers, on learning about my wheelchair push, asked me to say a few words about my accident and the Injured Jockeys Fund. This proved to be a fruitful evening as there was a collection for the push that came to £500, a sum matched by the other two regional managers.

Raising money for a charity that I become involved with gives me particular pleasure, be it the Injured Jockeys' Fund, Riding for the Disabled or the Midland Spinal Unit - which prepared me so well for life after my confrontation with the ground on the landing side of the last hurdle at Bangor.

Moments of Joy

If time could stand still in our moments of joy
Letting us capture them in a glass jar,
Stand them up side by side;
A constant reminder
Of the joy in our lives.

Then in quiet times
We could close our eyes and smile,
Stretching it out for many a mile.
With laughter, with love, with party glow
Our moments of joy we'd keep on show.
Then in darkness when we open our bag of woe
The jars would be there just to make sure,
That we could still make our own choice;
Balance the scales
Cry or rejoice.

I feel there is no choice for me
The scales won't balance
You see.
For my jars of joy far out-weigh
The bag of woe
On any day.

CHAPTER SEVEN

OSWESTRY HOME FROM HOME

I wonder how many people would love to go back to the place where they had broken their neck - or should I say where they were unavoidably detained. The first morning I woke up in that Oswestry Hospital I could not possibly have perceived how dear the market town and its people would become to me. After three weeks I was asked whether, when I was more stable, I would like to move to Lodge Moor Hospital in Sheffield - which is the area hospital for Newmarket. This would also bring me closer to my family's home in Yorkshire. "No, I was quite happy where I was, thank you."

I was extremely lucky because two miles down the road from the hospital at Pentre David lived my riding colleague Diana Jones and her family. I had frequently met the late Arthur Jones, his wife, Isobel, and daughter, Vicky, at the races. I didn't know their other daughter, Alex (but I do now!). They were wonderful, as was Vicky's friend, Sue Roberts - one or other of them would visit daily often bringing smoked salmon sandwiches or anything else I desired. The Jones' have played a major part and I will be forever grateful for their continued friendship.

Then, of course, there are the rugby boys, now what am I going to tell you about them? The stories I could regale - you wouldn't believe the half of it! I had met a bunch of guys that would turn out to be great friends. Big, tough physical characters who are kind and caring. Pussycats!

They're not laughing now - I can tell you! I have seen most of them at least twice a year ever since. Over the years we have spent numerous nights of frivolity in the Wynnstay Hotel and latterly the Sweeney Hall. Sean Evans the manager and co-owner of the Sweeney is given plenty of warning when I am coming to stay.

I feel that the impact of just how much the whole scenario of being left disabled, miles away from my close friends, was only realised a few years ago. I had never felt abandoned in Oswestry, in a way the Jones' and the boys had adopted me.

Ironically, in the throes of 1990, Diana Jones had invited me to stay at Pentre David when I told her that a break from Newmarket was much needed. "You can come and train with me and the boys at the rugby club." We even flirted with the idea of work riding in America for the winter. Both really appealed to me but neither happened as a new contact was made riding a few jumpers for trainer Ray Bostock. Once again the hunger and hope to ride winners took precedence.

The first year I came home from hospital I was determined to carry on with the usual functions that had been a part of my life. That summer I had a barbecue and five of the boys came to - not intentionally - wreck my house. A series of incidents were started five minutes after they entered Becklyn. Brett Hollywell opened a can of beer in the lounge and, yes, you've guessed - it squirted all over the place. He soon had his tee-shirt whipped off by one of my ladies (Nancy) who had it washed, dried and ready to wear almost immediately. Then Glynn Jones sat down heavily in one of my small armchairs and we heard it break. Robin Chilton took great delight in their misfortunes. Even when they went outside and Johnny Rees and Frank Logsdail started throwing a rugby ball about, Nancy's husband Alan started to run backwards as the ball was hurled into the air. "This one's mine," he managed to get out, before crashing into the bird table which also broke!

They came prepared with sleeping bags as they were all staying in the lounge. I told them not to break anything else! Before they were quite settled Brett, on deciding it was very warm, went to open the patio door. Not realising that in England we have modern tilt and turn windows and doors, he moved the handle into its tilt position, and thought he'd broken it as it came towards him. He stood there supporting it fearing it was going to fall in further. He pleaded with the others for help but they just laughed and left him holding it and said, "She is going to go mad!" Eventually his arms gave way and as it only dropped another degree, they thought that was even more hilarious as he pushed it back realising with plenty of expletives that it tilted as well as sliding open. In the morning they took great delight in telling me all this - raucously impersonating Brett!

They asked if they would ever be invited to come and stay again. They were and they did.

The next year was - oh yes, my memory is a bit hazy here. I remember them singing 'Goodnight Sweetheart' as I was tucked up in bed but I can't recall six of them stripped to the waist singing Bob Marley songs. I must have dreamt that!

Whenever I'm planning a visit to Oswestry, first I ring Vicky Jones and tell her, then she warns Sean at the Sweeney and books my accommodation. My next call is to Robin to round all the lads up. It's a good excuse for them to get together and have a catch-up with each other as well as me.

They have naturally gone their separate ways, time never standing still - the rugby club training nights are now mainly occupied twice a week by younger blood. Most of the 1991 players knocked out by injury only attend on occasions to cast a knowing eye and help prop the bar up!

It was early February '98 when I rang Robin and told him that BBC East wanted to do a documentary on me. For this, the director needed to film me out for dinner with friends and as we were spending the Friday filming at the hospital, and Saturday morning book signing in the town and then on to Bangor racecourse, Friday night would be an ideal time. I wanted him to ask Frank, Glynn, Brett, Platty and Trev, with girlfriends or not as the case may be, if they were free on that particular night. The first thing I heard down the telephone was a hearty laugh followed by "Do they know what they are letting themselves in for?" "No, I thought we'd surprise them!" I had already asked the Jones' and Sue Roberts. Sue had been my personal beautician for the duration of my stay in hospital. Broken neck or not a girl's got to try and look presentable!

The three man crew followed me to Oswestry (the start of a very long weekend) where I had a meeting with Mr El Masry, one of the country's top spinal injury consultants, and fund-raising manager Gwilym Owen, about the progress the Spiney Appeal Fund was making. Clive Dunn (the director) hadn't planned on filming so far afield but the meeting and dinner with my Oswestry friends was very relevant for my story. Mr El Masry likes me to go onto the wards and it was an ideal opportunity to show me having a chat with patients who have been injured and face the rest of their days in a wheelchair. This is my least favourite job, not because I don't want to help but many people feel they need to address what has happened to them in their own way and don't want some 'Know It All' coming along telling them that they can do this, that or the other. I never push people to talk to me, I just say "Your zest for life should not stop."

I know what it is like for them; I've been there. There are some who want to know everything that I can help them with. So, I help a few and maybe, in time, the aforementioned ones will keep living the life they have sadly ended up with.

I warned Janet, my helper, that my night would become day! And it did. Seventeen of us sat down for dinner and Clive kindly put £50 behind the bar. After the initial few pints for the boys, it was red wine until the singing was over. They all have great singing voices, especially Frank, Trev and Robin. When dinner was over it was getting on for 10.30pm. Clive came and apologised as he had been held up with the day's procedures. It was so late he thought I must be very tired and would want to go to bed, as tomorrow was going to be another hectic day with the two book signing appointments and the Bangor racecourse visit. Robin came to push me through to the foyer where more bottles of wine were being consumed. He overheard Clive's concern about it being late and tiring for me, scoffing at both comments "Late! It's not late, man, and she's not tired." Clive looked surprised and I assured him I was far from tired.

Robin enquired whether the camera was off, the reply was "Yes" as the crew joined us for a few drinks. "Right everyone, we can all act normal now the camera's off," he announced and a loud cheer went up! Jeff, the cameraman and Robin, the soundman, sat down with the lads and soon there were all kinds of funny stories being passed around. They managed to stay up for a few songs. The renditions usually start with 'Leroy Brown' led by Frank and everyone joins in for the chorus. Clive and Jeff wondered how I was going to get up the long steep flight of stairs to my room. " The boys carry me," I said matter of factly. They pointed out that we'd all had a few. "Makes life more interesting, don't you think," I teased, telling them that this was not the first or the last time that I would put my life in their hands. They said goodnight and when they reached half way Robin shouted, "If you hear a loud clatter and a few cheers don't worry - we'll have just dropped her!"

Once the singing starts you can safely say that the earliest your bed is going to see you is shortly before the milkman appears. The form is loud and lucid to mellow and melancholy. My favourites are 'My Way' (for obvious reasons) and 'Love Story' (Frank), 'Peaceful Easy Feeling' (Frank and Trev) 'Willy McBride' (Trev), two lines of 'Nessun Dorma' (Robin - well he is very loud!) and 'Knocking on Heaven's Door' (Trev's brother Johnny mostly sang at my barbecues but is still worth a mention!) The highlight of these singing sessions for all - and I must admit Glynn and I are rather good at this particular song - is, 'Streets Of London'. We have been known for our temperamental ways, I - as any diva will tell you, have to have a perfect ambience before performing. Our singing usually wraps up the evening that has all too soon become the early hours of another day because we are quite simply tone deaf and everyone makes for the nearest exit! (Painful as Diana Jones puts it). On this particular evening the boys decided that they would join in thus drowning out our voices (there were other guests to consider) and Trev had leant over to me earlier and whispered, "Shaz, shut up - your singing's crap, stick to the poetry." Fact.

Janet had me washed, dressed and in my chair by 9am the next morning, then, as prearranged, Sue arrived with rollers, tongs and make-up. "Can't have you looking like a slap head, eh Shazza." As the hair was curling nicely Sue put some make-up on me, asking what time we finally came to bed. It was around 3 am but I wasn't feeling any after effects, in fact I was frighteningly bright!

"Clive, you worry too much," I told him as he anxiously asked if I'd be okay for the rest of the day. If the filming at Bangor didn't take place it would ruin the whole concept of the programme. Robin appeared more than a trifle hung-over and, thinking I'd be even worse, was surprised to see me up and ready with hair and make-up done. I ribbed him saying he was far too old for such a late night and was he still up to helping us out for the book signings? "Oh, I'll get you back for that."

I was in position at 10.30am on the dot at WH Smiths on 14th February 1998, six years to the day that I'd flown home for good, courtesy of Sheikh Mohammed's helicopter. Both *Jump Jockeys* and *Nil Desperandum* were on display. The truth, I thought, is definitely stranger than fiction. A few of the nurses from the hospital came in with their friends, as did other locals. It had not been a wasted visit and I was pleased with the sales. Clive finished filming the book signing and then he confirmed our meeting time of 2.30pm at Bangor. Glynn appeared briefly and whilst he and Robin milled around the far side of the shop it gave me a perfect opportunity to select some Valentine cards before moving on to the Wynnstay.

Robin took over pushing me down the High Street and left Janet with Vicky to carry the rest of the books. Jan was busy shopping for that evening's dinner as Trev, Platty, Glynn, Sarah and I were invited. The chair stopped suddenly in the middle of the pavement and Robin bent over, put the brakes on about 20 metres from the Wynnstay and began to walk away, stopping within earshot. He lent against some railings grinning under the pretence of not knowing me, I gasped "What are you doing?" He ignored me. Abandoned in this position, people were having to walk around me - and I was getting some very odd looks but not one offer of any help! I told him to "Come and get me, NOW!" He'd got his own back - point taken - score even.

The Wynnstay was packed for Saturday lunches and they had put a table in the adjoining conservatory for me to display and sign my books. Arthur and Isobel were there in the main bar with a gathering of friends but I was surprised to see Trev, Martin (ex rugby fitness trainer) and his son Spencer waiting for me - "Ahh, my first three customers." And they didn't let me down. We spoke briefly about the previous evening, Trev remarking that we hadn't sung at all - I reminded him of what he'd said to me the night before. Martin gasped. Trev apologised sitting down next to me - forgiven as always.

I must admit I was flagging by the time we met up with trainer Alan Bailey at Bangor. It's amazing how eerie a deserted racecourse feels. I told Clive that I used to be Alan's assistant trainer and asked him if he thought I could be a good assistant director as I had all but assisted him for the last week. He said I'd make a good assistant director; I smiled and then he added, "But not for me!"

We began to make our way over the course and down towards the last hurdle - the place where my life had been changed in a split second forever. Clive, Jeff and Robin (the soundman) searched for the best place to shoot the required footage. I could see how hard it was for Alan. This was the man who had set me on my way, gave me the chance to pursue my dreams and fuelled my hungry ambition. In all but blood he'd taken on the mantle of a father, caring so much that he had tried to guide me in the right direction but, at the end of the day, I made my own decisions - I always had.

"What do you feel as we approach the hurdle?" Alan asked. I paused before answering, "Nothing, really."

I didn't feel a sense of foreboding, anxiety, dread or fear as I was being pushed towards the last hurdle where I had fallen with my horse on that Friday. I didn't even feel sad - the smell of the grass and woodiness of the hurdle struck me, their familiarity tweaking my memory and taking me back to a place where I belonged. I'd been there; wrapped up in the hubbub of excitement with its colourful language and barrage of noise - thundering hooves sparing no man or woman whose time had come. The silence was almost as exciting - or was it just being there?

The filming went well and although I had by now become very tired I still had to go for dinner at Robin and Jan's. Janet suggested that I ring them to say I was too tired but I replied, "I can't do that, Janet, it was my idea!" She looked very pale and I asked if she was okay, she said she was but thought she may be getting flu. "Well, I definitely won't be late tonight," I assured her.

Janet dropped me off at Robin and Jan's and went back to the Sweeney, I would 'phone her when I was ready. At twenty to nine we were eating dessert and I'd had all the good intentions of ringing her at 10.30pm at the latest - then, beyond my control, the singing started. My tiredness abated. It was 11pm when Janet arrived to pick me up and it was going on for 3am when Sean, from the Sweeney, rang to ask how long I would be - as he was waiting to help lift me up the stairs. I didn't want the night to end, this is my downfall - I never want the nights to end. Do I skate on thin ice or what?

We had a fantastic Christmas party in November '99 and it was also a surprise anniversary celebration for Jan. Robin and I had been plotting furtively, arranging with Sean to use the function room upstairs. I smiled to myself, as the boys were about to lift me up the long winding staircase, Robin took the back handles and then without hesitation Frank and Trev took hold of the curved bar that is part of the footplates, in front of me. It was the first time Trev had helped to lift me up the stairs since his accident - he was physically well on the mend. We said goodbye to the 90s in proper fashion. Toasting them for all the enjoyable times and cursing them for the deprivation some of us had suffered - yet saluting the fact that we would be forever stronger as friends - as people.

Then it was down to serious mickey taking. After I had left hospital Frank sent me a tape of him singing quite a few songs - and promised me that when he got Trev and Johnny together, there would be a few more. He had also promised a tape of the full fifteen (that's rugby players) singing 'Peaceful, Easy Feeling'. Robin asked me if Frank had sent me the other tape yet? Frank then covered his face and I (in my best singing voice) replied, "I'm Still Waiting ...oh, no - Diana Ross sings that!"

They don't allow me to get away with anything either - even though you shouldn't mock the afflicted. My attempts at joining in their equivalent of singing scales as "Baa, Baa, Baa" are shot down in flames!

It was also on this particular night that Robin told me that when the film crew came to Oswestry, Clive (the director) said he had travelled the world but never had he witnessed a scene in a hotel lobby to compare with the one we provided!

My own personal song for this band of friends (I told Robin - after trying to sing it) is Clifford T. Ward's 'Sometimes When We Touch' because of the lines 'The honesty's too much, I want to hold you till the fear in me subsides...'

Even after all this time they still make the effort to either join me for dinner or at least have a drink and a quick hello whenever I am in the vicinity. For reasons like this Oswestry has become a bolt-hole for me. On many occasions we have revelled in each other's company - partying late into the night - ending up like a big kid's impromptu slumber party. Bodies strewn on floor and furniture drift off to sleep - too late for taxis, too early for breakfast - and I lay listening to the peaceful breathing drawing comfort from the fact that I am not alone.

Annual Christmas Dinner Party with (from left to right) David Thom, Gee Armytage, Richard Phillips, the late Alison Thom and myself (1998).

Me and Joss Drake (Christmas 2000).

Riding 'Fiefdom' with help from Andy Young (1998).

The wheelchair push - 25 miles completed (1998).

Breathe but don't talk! Scuba dive practice at Mar-y-sol (1999).

Out at sea preparing to scuba dive (1999).

Throw me in…

Feeling free, floating free at Mar-y-sol (1999).

Me with Shirley Marshall (left), Janet Boston (centre) and Linda O'Hara (right) at Mar-y-sol (2001).

Rebecca Hewitt (left), myself (centre) and Barbara Towler (right) (2001).
PHOTOGRAPH COURTESY OF D. (TICH) COOMBES

In tandem with Danny Smith (1999).

120 mph - air cool.

All back on terra firma.

Family relieved. From left to right: David, Justine, mum, Kelly and Barry (1999).

Back to work in my office, wheels firmly on the ground (2000).

Richard Phillips and I at the Lesters (2001).

Injured Jockeys' holiday at Mar-y-sol (2001).
PHOTOGRAPH COURTESY OF ED WHITAKER

Time Is The Thief

Woke up again too soon the morning has come.
Motionless I lie
Still breathing from pictures of yesterday
Time is the thief
Seeping my life away.

If only to catch just one drop of all the elation
We've come to share on many a night
Friends together in laughter
Raucous till the break of morning light.
Talk we talk of everything
That is wrong and how we'd make it all so right,
Not realising that time is the thief
Taking the hours whilst we are in full flight.
Singing from 'Leroy Brown' to the very soul of 'Willy McBride'
'Love Story' and 'Knocking on Heaven's Door'
So pleased you are all by my side.
We will never say goodbye to 'American Pie'
All joining in for there is no need to hide.
Then it's 'Peaceful Easy Feeling' and we all close our eyes
Imagining the place while time steals away our lives.
'The Streets of London' no sooner said than done
There's laughter whilst this song by the tuneless ones is sung.
We let the very source of joy and love
Flow through our veins
With wine and song always the mainstay.

Closing our eyes too soon we have to kiss goodnight
Not wanting sleep
Still tingling from the love of what we say
Time is the thief
Stealing our lives away.

CHAPTER EIGHT

PUSH OFF INTO THE DEEP

I was pleased when I came home from holiday in 1998. There were two reasons: one, I had lost a stone in weight since the previous October and, secondly, for the rest of the summer I would be able to concentrate on the wheelchair push that I was going to do in aid of the Midland Spinal Unit. I'd started the outline planning in January when I first spoke to the Clerk of the Course, Major Webster, but there was still a lot of outstanding work.

I soon had to get to grips and focus on the wheelchair push. Together with a good friend, Keith Holland, we set the wheels in motion. He played a vital part in the whole operation.

First of all Keith and I mapped out the following letter:

The Robert Jones and Agnes Hunt
Orthopaedic and District Hospital NHS Trust
President: HRH The Duchess of Kent
Oswestry, Shropshire SY10 7AG

«Trainer's Name»
«Address 1»

June 1998

Dear

On Friday 31st July, as part of 'Sharron Murgatroyd Day' at Bangor races, I am to undertake a sponsored wheelchair push. Seven years ago to this date I was paralysed in a fall at Bangor, and this is my contribution to the Appeal Fund for the Midlands Centre for Spinal Injuries at Oswestry. The plan is to take the exact route from the last hurdle at Bangor to the Spinal Unit at Oswestry via Wrexham Maelor Hospital, that I travelled, by ambulance, on that fateful day. It is about 25 miles.

The Midlands Spinal Unit is a world-renowned centre of excellence for the treatment of spinal injuries. The Centre is currently accommodated in hospital buildings from the 1920s, which are outdated and do not have the standard of necessary facilities of a Spinal Injuries Centre such as sufficient privacy and bathroom arrangements. These requirements are of particular importance to patients who have suffered such a traumatic change to their capabilities and mental outlook. It is as a mark of my appreciation of the wonderful treatment that I received there that I decided to undertake this 'push'. I wanted to repay them, in some small way, for all the help and encouragement that they provided.

As I hope to raise a substantial sum for the fund I am writing to members of the racing community seeking sponsorship. If you would agree to sponsor me for a minimum of 20p per mile - a total of £5 - it would enable me to make a really worthwhile contribution to the Spinal Unit Appeal on behalf of Racing.

Yours sincerely

Sharron

Sharron Murgatroyd

The following have agreed to be Patrons of
The Midlands Centre for Spinal Injuries Appeal:
Lady Masham, Lord Gowrie, Sharron Murgatroyd,
Denis Amiss MBE, Rupert Moon and Maj. John Warburton-Lee.
Charity No. 1058878

There was a rapid response and Keith was soon banking plenty of cheques. It was overwhelming - racing people once again coming together to offer their support. I had to ring the post office as we were a little worried about my postbox being at the end of the drive - and request delivery straight to the house, which was no problem.

A 'phone call to my old boss, Alan Bailey, proved fruitful and he asked his owners if they would sponsor a race in my name. His loyalty and unstinting support once again championed the cause.

The way the event escalated was astounding and soon I was inundated with letters flooding in from the general public wishing me luck in my venture. I received a letter from a Mr Osborne, who had a framed front page copy of Frankie Dettori's seven-wins-in-a-day as featured in the Sporting Life which he wanted to donate, suggesting it was auctioned. His father lived at Moulton, Newmarket and Keith collected it. I rang Frankie and asked if he would autograph it, and as usual he was more than obliging.

I also had to ring round a lot of the jockeys to ask them, if they were booked to ride at Bangor, would they be willing to start off the push after the last race on Friday 31st July? They were a little surprised to hear of my plan to start at the last hurdle for the first leg, which was to be the casualty unit in Wrexham, a distance of seven miles. The second leg was to take place the next day and I had to find willing point-to-point riders in the area to start me off, then the rugby boys would meet us half way and we'd take it from there. Peter Rossdale had kindly offered his services but, sadly, his wife was ill at the time so he recruited three of his vets: Deidre Ringer, Mike Shepherd and Pete Ramzan.

I rang John Wilson who was the area point-to-point manager and he kindly offered to try and find me some riders who would be willing to participate in this charity run. He was a great help and found five fit, willing and able jockeys who would meet me at 12 o'clock outside the Mealor Hospital to begin the 18 mile haul. These were: Anthony Evans, John Barlow, Simon Prior, Neil Gittings and the late Mike Worthington. I was delighted, for that meant I would have at least twelve people to push me back to the Orthopaedic Hospital.

My good friend, Gee Armytage, organised six pushers who would definitely go all the way to Wrexham on the Friday evening - I would have to wait to hear from any of the other jockeys as to their availability.

Gwlymn Owen, the Appeal Director, helped map out a route and, on the day, he would head what turned out to be a convoy of cars! By the first week in July everything was in place, the Racing Channel would be at Bangor that day and had offered plenty of coverage; all I had to do was start training.

I could lie and say I trained hard for the wheelchair push but, unfortunately after feeling unwell for a week (hoping it would soon pass), with ten days to go before the push, I had to have the doctor in. I'd had a virus and then a mild dose of chickenpox was diagnosed which made me feel horrid. Not as horrid as Keith's face - with three days to go he asked me why I was still lounging in my recliner (more concerned for the push than me, I might add). There was even talk of finding a 'look-a-like'! Needless to say, at the twelfth hour when Janet, Joan and I had arrived at Bangor that old surge of adrenaline helped me through what turned out to be a brilliant weekend.

A hectic day ensued; Sally Kenyon (who with Peter Ockeston had played a pivotal roll in organising this day) had photocopied my original letter and sent it to her many contacts who were very generous. They also arranged a fund-raising marquee. I had lunch on arrival and met many of the people sponsoring me. There were two separate interviews with Gordon Brown of the Racing Channel. In the first one I told Gordon that I hoped to raise £10,000. As the coverage went out people were ringing Bangor asking where to send sponsor money and Keith faxed the racecourse saying we had reached £13,000!

My former valet Pat Taylor also had a whip-round in the weighing room. He and his wife Sheila had been marvellous over the years and Pat often sent flowers from different weighing rooms around the country when I was in hospital which were always signed 'Love From the Lads and Lasses'. We looked at each other, both knowing how very different it all was at this time of the day - seven years ago.

Owners, trainers and racegoers were coming up to me, handing over notes. It seemed that nearly every person on the racecourse that day didn't know what a deep pocket was!

I was very carried away by mid-afternoon and every radio station or press interview was met with a polite request to put some money in the coffers first! The bumper crowd was eight or nine deep round the parade ring for the auction of the signed 'Magnificent Seven Winners'. The auctioneer kept it lively and after much bantering it would go home with a Myra Stanyer for £800. She had heard about the push on the radio that morning and decided to come to the races as she had a vested interest. At first I didn't recognise her as I helped hand over her purchase but then realised she was the mother of a guy called Peter, who had been in hospital at the same time as me. Peter broke his neck in a car accident and was lucky to walk again - the crash leaving him with one paralysed arm.

In the second interview with Gordon, live for the Racing Channel (who had given the whole day major coverage), I told him the event had spiralled beyond even one of my wildest dreams - we were getting on for £20,000 and I hadn't even started the push! The last race was won by 'So Keen', trained by Alan Bailey - there could not have been a more fitting end to this day's racing. As I said in my first book: sheer unadulterated magic!

A large gathering of the racegoers stayed to watch the start of the push and even though Tony McCoy, Chris Maude and Tony Dobbin had pressing engagements, they all came down to the last hurdle. Tony McCoy grabbed hold of the chair as if it was one trained by Martin Pipe and immediately tipped it up on the back wheels. He certainly knew how to handle the wheels as we sped away from the last hurdle, setting the pace (which took everyone by surprise) and precedence for the rest of the journey. The first changeover was just outside the racecourse, Tony

Dobbin and then Chris pushed until McCoy had collected his car.

I was on my way - destination Wrexham on a Friday evening with Gee Armytage, Michael Caulfield, Carl Llewelyn, Sean Curran, Chris Webb, Johnny Kavanagh and Glen Tormey, all keeping up the pace - not to be outdone by McCoy. How mad is that? Someone had thrust a bottle of champagne into Janet's hand for me as she and Joan jumped into my car in pursuit of the runaway wheelchair and jockeys. A convoy of cars soon built up so any one of the running pushers could have a rest.

Gee came running upsides and asked if I needed a drink as we were about to face the first hill, where I thought we were going to have a stop. The next minute Gee pushed my plastic glass into my hand. "There you are, Shazza." We obviously weren't stopping and yes, it was champagne and no, I didn't spill a drop!

It took just under the hour to do 7 miles which was really good going - I think the boys were on a promise! With the first leg accomplished it was back to the Sweeney Hotel where Gee, Michael and Carl joined us for a bar snack. We'd all had a long day and as I went off to bed they faced the long journey back to Lambourn - camaraderie undiminished.

I resumed at the Maelor Hospital on Saturday and by midday I had met all the point-to-point jockeys and the three Newmarket vets (who had made the long journey just for this event). I told them of the pace that had been set the evening before but, obviously, as our remaining mileage was 18 - I quite understood the need for a steadier speed. "If they can do it, we can do it"; a competitive spirit emerged from them. So, dead on time and right on pace I was pushed away from the Maelor - destination Oswestry.

We had some collecting tins but were regarded by other motorists mostly as an inconvenience as we held up the traffic at times. Some were quite irate and not even a shake of the charity tin warranted turning the window down. If I were to do anything like that again, there would have to be some kind of sign and posters advertising the fact that a charity event was taking place. Gwilym's advert on his car was not enough.

Every time there was a changeover I had to ask, "Who's pushing now?" They would reply and we'd have a chat - for as long as their breath held out! I would collect the accolade at the end of the day but at least I could keep them amused, as I didn't run out of breath at all! The rugby boys were set to meet us at a village called St Martins, at our rendezvous time of 3pm. Their late arrival on the scene was because of the Oswestry Show where some were actually showing animals or helping with the organisation and the others were in the beer tent.

I told all the pushers that the boys were meeting us so that would take some pressure off them and they could have a rest. The convoy of cars was even greater than the night before and even though it rained a little it wasn't enough to dampen our spirits. So much so that we were ahead of schedule and this allowed us to have an unplanned pub stop. I rang Robin Chilton and told him where we were and he couldn't believe what progress we had made. Robin had one more prize bull to show and then he'd be on his way - hopefully with a few others. However, as they were all in the beer tent at that precise moment, I would understand if a couple of them didn't turn up. This was especially obvious after talking to one of them who told me to come to the beer tent straight after I'd finished - and I could hear a barrage of well-wishers shouting in the background. I didn't have to have O levels to realise the numbers were diminishing by the pint! But it was their annual outing that started when they were kids.

Meanwhile, back in the pub, another round had been ordered as St Martins was only ten minutes away. After refreshments it was back on the road, before we pulled into a lay-by and I decided to give the rugby boys five more minutes to arrive before carrying on. As I was speaking to a photographer, who had unexpectedly turned up, I heard a voice asking, "Where have you been?" I told the man, "That sounds just like my mum," and the voice said, "It is your mum!" With my brother Mark and his wife, Helen, they had been looking for us for an hour or more. Unfortunately it was while we were in the pub that they had passed by three times, not thinking for one moment that we would make such an unscheduled stop. Mark wasn't very amused as he had suggested stopping at the pub for a drink but my mum was more interested in finding me!

Just as we were about to give up on the rugby lads, and the point-to-point jockeys and vets were relishing the idea of conquering the biggest hill that we had come to face (amazing what a couple of pints can do), they arrived, Glynn and Brett first closely followed by Robin.

We were on a small downhill slope before the steep incline, where it was quite possible that two pairs of arms and legs would be needed. After a brief discussion it was Brett who would start pushing. Apart from a couple of annoyed looks everything had gone smoothly - but within a couple of minutes Brett had me nearly head butting the kerb. There were gasps from my other pushers, with an exclamation of, "I thought you knew what you were doing!" Robin was laughing as he sat me back in the chair and Brett calmly retrieved his cigarettes and lighter that had jumped out of his shirt pocket as he began to run - hence the sudden unprepared stop and jolt as the front wheels hit the kerb!

"What have I done to upset you, Brett?" I asked in an amused voice when I'd regained my posture, then Robin butted in, "You've only been here two minutes, Brett, and nearly caused an accident, that must be a record - even for you!"

Up until now our rattling of charity tins hadn't gone too well but things were about to take a turn. Robin stood in the centre of the road and began physically stopping the traffic. "Stand and deliver, your money or your life." The vets and jockeys couldn't believe his cheek and audacity.

My arrival at the Orthopaedic Hospital was a bit of an anti-climax; only two people were there to see the triumphant return and they were my loyal supporters - Isobel Jones and her daughter, Vicky. Mr El Masry had put on tea and sandwiches in the Unit's meal room and although I would have loved to have gone to the Oswestry Show beer tent, the Sweeney Hotel was a more sensible option. Our efforts were well rewarded and I was astonished when 2 months later the total of the Sharron Murgatroyd Day at Bangor (including wheelchair push) raised £40,000.

On 16 September 1998 I started to write a novel. I gave myself a year to write it and a year for it to be processed. My plan was to have it launched in 2000. Ideas came thick and fast and I wrote two strong chapters. I had what I thought was a good beginning and I'd even planned the end - which would contain a big twist (nobody would have seen that one coming). Peter Bloomfield, who had been my working colleague at Alan Bailey's, rang one day as I was working on this new project. We ended up spending the next two hours on the 'phone, plotting and planning out a near perfect and plausible story. Unfortunately the middle part was weak - very weak...

I persevered, sorting the advice from both John Francome and Jim McGrath, but after a series of disheartening events - twice losing different amounts of words ranging from three to five hundred, that I had struggled to write on the computer - I decided to shelve it. A renewed attempt after speaking to Jim McGrath in November '99 still found me wanting. I had tried to tell a plausible story for just over a year. As Christmas approached the forthcoming novel was no more.

There were other reasons as well; the combination of my inadequacy to please one of my main critics - Keith - although Janet was enthusiastic, and the onset of what some people call writer's block. That being said, I don't look upon myself as a writer. I felt the reason for not being able to write a novel was because I didn't have what it takes.

After five years of writing and all the rigmarole that goes with it I was finished. I could trot out the poetry ten to the dozen - but there doesn't seem to be many people that interested. I was still being asked to do my local WI talks that had become a regular feature over the past couple of years. I'd sell a few books and in payment received a donation for the Injured Jockeys' Fund. It was easy; I only had to talk about myself and it saved boring my friends!

The decision to update my word processor was prompted by Andy who, in addition to his own, takes great care in keeping my stable yard spick and span. Andy and Keith both have Windows '98 and so as not to be left behind I took possession of an all-singing, all-dancing internet computer, which came just at the right time. I realised there were lots of other interesting things for me to do - with my window to the world I could spend my time becoming computer literate (ha, ha).

I have a great set-up in my office (which was my old bedroom). I face the wall, which is adorned by many pictures of friends, and my racing photographs that I can see when a stretching of the neck upwards is needed. All my telephone numbers are on display and I am very independent, with 'phone and music under my control (very important if I feel the need to headbang with Bowie). The window to my right overlooks the paddocks and lets in plenty of light so I have the perfect place in which to use my brain!

I enjoyed Christmas and looked forward to making full use of my new toy. We (Andy, Keith and I) drove my poor mother mad as we compared notes, had heated discussions and kept ringing each other up to see if our e-mails had arrived - with attachments or not. Some days I had a job to even get on my own computer as Andy and Keith were on it before I'd cleaned my teeth!

I was lucky to have them around as I needed plenty of assistance and whenever I got stuck I'd make a 'phone call to Andy (the Riding Instructor), Keith (the Egg Man) or David Male (the Teacher) for information. Thank goodness I didn't have anyone else or I could have been implicated in the biggest 'racehorse doping farce' of recent times with some of my former colleagues!

Andy and Keith would show me the right way to do the simplest things but that was the problem - at times I was unbelievably thick! One of them would come and with a couple of mouse clicks solve whatever I was having difficulty with. I was definitely in the dumb and dumber category. This was much to Keith's annoyance and the air was often very blue in my office but we certainly kept my ladies amused!

I continued my physio with Gabrielle on Tuesday and Friday mornings, not so much for strength as I felt I'd reached my full potential but for the all important passive movement of legs and feet. My arms did a bit of work and I stood up in my standing frame. Then if my two friends had not already accessed my computer and put a 'new program on that I would need' or "We're just having a look at something", I had a fair chance of using it myself. Of course they were only trying to help me and boy did I need help. If they told me once they told me a thousand times and I would say, "Yes, I know that bit Andy" - and Keith would say, "If you know stop ringing us up." They used to get really mad with me and I did with them. But it didn't stop them helping!

Obviously this still worked around all Saturday racing and any major mid-week racing on TV - and I would go racing occasionally.

Then of course as I played around with my software - I had a good idea. Well, other people were doing it and with the help of Dave (the Teacher) I wanted to jump on the 'dot com' bandwagon. The biggest attraction for me was to build my own website. It would be racing orientated and I had plenty of information, facts, notes and background to work with. In theory it looked great (just like at school in cookery class when you would write down the recipe for cakes in your neatest handwriting). My creative imagination was full steam ahead!

Dave and I started working - my ideas - his brains! It began to take shape with the main picture of me riding 'Beechwood Cottage' - animated! This wasn't going to be a wishy-washy site. The title in a wide format ran continuously under the galloping horse to the instrumental sounds of 'All the Young Dudes' which I'd downloaded from the Bowie site. This was just for effect - for when Keith came round to have a look, after not wanting anything to do with it!

I started to do my homework, checking out other sites that had been already established. They were smooth looking and I was bringing in too many colours when it was still in its embryonic stage. The theory was good and it wasn't a wishy-washy site, but it was like the cakes came out at school - tacky.

When the Injured Jockeys' Fund holidays come round, I leave Andy in charge of looking after Becklyn. Much to his chagrin I type out a list of 'destructions'. This particular year the first one was 'You And Keith Are Not To Operate My Computer For YOUR Internet Usage!' To make sure that they adhered to my instructions, I asked Janet to unplug my internet connection and push it around the back of my desk. "That will stop them, they won't bother crawling under the desk to plug it back in."

Although I was looking forward to going on holiday, the sad death of Peter Rossdale's wife, Jill, cast a shadow. Together with Peter, she had been enthusiastic and supportive about my work. Her funeral was to take place whilst I was in Tenerife but although Serena Oxley (my almoner) represented me I felt I should have been there. Serena joined us for the last week of the holiday and whilst I rested on a sunbed she told me all about the church service. I was both surprised and honoured that Peter had concluded the commemoration card with my poem 'Moments of Joy'.

With the full glare of sun on my face I closed my eyes with mixed emotions, the vision of her smiling face seemed to appear with not only absolute clarity but also approval. Whenever I think of her my impression is always of her kind and smiling face.

The year before was the first time I had experienced snorkelling.

Serena thought I'd like it and I borrowed her snorkel after finding out that, together with Janet and Michelle's help, it was possible for me to go on my front in the water. I wanted to do it - I like trying different activities, it's a good thing. I liked the water on my face and had been shaking my head from side to side. We had even managed to do a width of the pool underwater. Janet had held her hand under my chin and would lift it up for me to have a breath of air, but subsequently when I came to snorkel I could do it with my eyes open and breathe at the same time. Janet and Michelle put the gear on me and with one each side I slipped down through the water. They brought me up after breathing in and out a few times, making sure I was okay. 'Yeah, great, even though the view isn't.'

Now what is the first rule of anything where hearing or speech is not viable? Everybody knows that SOS - formerly CQD - is a signal for distress, a sign or gesture. CQD was a general call to all vessels, indicating the vessel sending, is in distress and requires immediate assistance. The Titanic used CQD as it was then still in common use, although it had been officially replaced by the well known SOS - chosen specifically to be easily and instantly recognisable in Morse code - 'dit dit dit, dah dah dah, dit dit dit.'

It was remiss of us to completely overlook safety procedures in the enthusiasm of my second submergence into the water. I could hear them speaking through the air pipe although they were totally unaware of this. I was moving my left arm slowly through the water, in a vain attempt to swim but the right arm hung down and there was hardly any movement at all. Every time one of our party walked or wheeled by they enquired "Is that Sharron down there?" "Yes." "She looks to be enjoying it." "Yes, she is." After about ten minutes of looking at Janet's foot and hearing all the chat I'd had enough, so I tapped at Janet's leg. "I think she wants to move around a bit, Michelle." "Okay." Then one of the men said, "Is that Sharron down there?" "Yes." "Good, keep her down there for a bit longer!" I smiled to myself (he didn't know I could hear him) but as I did the air pipe popped out of my mouth.

I tapped at Janet's leg again - but she thought I wanted her to move around. So I started to move my head from side to side full of confidence that they would bring me up. Unaware my breathing apparatus was no longer doing its job, everybody around the pool thought I was enjoying myself immensely! I began waving my left arm back and forth more energetically and shaking my head as vigorously as I could. At last my distress signals worked and they brought me up. "Bleep, bleep...where have you been??" I managed to blurt out. "We thought you were waving, not drowning!"

We learnt two things that day - I should always have a signal like

Titanic's CQD distress call - and it obviously meant 'Come Quick Drowning.'

Every year it seems we have a new or amusing tale to tell; it had already been a really fun holiday. Together with Barbara and Andrew Towler (the 'Brig'), Jaquie Oliver (my old 'Comrade'), her fiance, Andrew, Rebecca Hewitt and her friend Jayne Green we'd had many a raucous night. They had also commented on my change of image and weight loss. So, the opportunity for us to go scuba diving was yet another added bonus. My previous encounter of being underwater had not put me off. We had to go in the pool first and if we were proficient (and didn't panic) we would be able to go out in the open sea - in full diving gear.

The practice in the pool was vital and although it was a bit of a struggle putting all the gear on, we managed. Once the inflatable jackets were pumped up, goggles in place and mouthpiece secure, the most important safety procedures were taught. A nod of my head for okay, when the instructor made an O with his thumb and finger, and a shake of the head if I wanted to resurface. I was pushed down into the pool - breathing in rhythm, the rhythm I knew all about - the same sort is required when riding a racehorse. The first sign was shown and I nodded. It was quite simply bliss. I almost felt as if I was on my own. I passed the test and could go in the sea. Fantabulous, I couldn't wait!

Rebecca, who had dived before, Jonathan and I flew the flag for the wheelchair brigade, as all the others were able-bodied. There was some concern about me going into the sea as it would be very cold and I had only been in hydrotherapy pools. The three almoners, including my own, Serena Oxley, who after all these years knew that my keenness to do anything wasn't easily thwarted, held back, as talk about me becoming hypothermic in the sea went on. It was such a hot day that the sand was burning the feet of those who could stand up!

Joan (my helper with Janet that year) was not so sure that I should be undertaking such an adventure. She was worried who would tell my mum if I had to be hospitalised. In her stance - hands on hips - after asking me if this was a good idea she eventually came out with the saying that will always stick, "Well, it's nothing to do with me."

"So you're worried I'll get cold then." "Yes." "Not worried that I could drown - who would break the news to my mum if her daughter drowned at sea?"

As Jonathan and Rebecca are both paraplegic they could manage with a bit of help, to put on their wetsuits. I, on the other hand, was laid out with many onlookers (wondering what the heck was going on there.) A blanket was placed on the walkway and, after a little discussion by the two instructors (in German), the wetsuit was turned inside out and they rolled it feet first, a couple of quick turns and it was on - they knew exactly what they were doing. I was a little apprehensive when the weight belt was put on. "Are you sure you're supposed to put all this lead in the belt?" I asked the diving instructor. Oh, yes, he was quite sure - I needed to be weighed down. I did enquire further whether anybody had put him up to anchoring me on the seabed!

I was first to be wheeled into the Atlantic, all instructions fixed firmly in my mind, then the next minute I was submerged. I must have gone down at least 30,000 fathoms - could even have been more… actually, it was only 18 feet but don't tell anybody, as this was still impressive enough for me to be known as 'The Deep Sea Diver'. It was a wonderful experience - seeing at first hand the many varied species of ocean life. I felt almost encapsulated within my own world, all I could hear was my breathing together with the bubbling sound of the air tanks. However, for all you Titanic fans I didn't see Jack! I'd like to swim with dolphins one day. That's dolphins, not sharks!

Unfortunately, prior to the scuba diving I had quite badly bruised the area of my bottom bone (ischium) on both sides. For eight years I had never had a problem with my skin - I was almost blasé about the warnings I had been given in hospital. I had stupidly taken my gel cushion off the borrowed electric chair because my feet were not touching the footplates. That sitting for two hours on the inadequate wheelchair seat would alter the course of my life for the next two years…

Gypsy Girl

I want to be the first thing you think of
In the morning when you wake,
I want to be with you in your sunset
Beside you at daybreak.
I want to be the reason for you living
The freedom in your soul
I want to be your friend and your lover
Someone there to hold.

Gypsy girl; I can give you gypsy dreams
See me dancing round the fire
With bare feet just wanting to be free.
I want to be the only one you reach for
When you're restless in your sleep,
I want to be the one you long for
The only one you want to keep.
I want to be the one in your heart
Even when times are bad
I want to be the one you run to
When you're feeling sad.

Gypsy girl; I can give you gypsy dreams
See me hold out my hand
Roaming free that's the gypsy girl in me.

CHAPTER NINE

FROM HIGH TO LOW

One evening on that same holiday, when we were telling each other what we would like to do, I said I'd love to try a parachute jump. Jonathan Haynes had done one a few years before and couldn't see any problem with me having a go. I had wanted to go parascending the previous year. However, after Jonathan, who can use his arms had been up, and Janet went up to do a dummy run (as if she was me and found the straps dug into her), Jonathan said without the use of my arms and hands to hold onto the harness, plus a not altogether reliable crew to catch my immobile legs on landing - I should stay on *terra firma*. I heeded their advice and reluctantly went for lunch instead. Much to Joan's joy!

When Jack Berry who had joined us for a week, heard me saying I'd do a parachute jump he asked me to do a sponsored skydive at his Open Day at the stables. He'd organise it all as the parachute club was only a few miles away. It would be on Sunday 1st August, the day before the ninth anniversary of my fall. The next morning a full inquiry was held but I assured everyone I did remember what I said - I was only mildly inebriated and nothing had changed in this particular warm light of the day.

The flight home after this holiday had aggravated the right-hand side of my bottom, in fact it was quite red. I would have to confine myself to bed rest until it went away and, as I'd found out from previous years, my body felt quite weak after the holiday and what with all that deep sea diving - who could blame it?

The red mark improved immensely and on the second day I was sitting up in bed for a couple of hours in the morning (to read the papers), afternoon (watch the racing) and evening to eat my dinner. I decided to give it one more day just to be on the safe side, then a couple of days in the pushy chair should see me resume normality in my electric Powertec 50, which gave me so much more independence. Unfortunately, as I was reading the papers I got the sensation in my arms and the cold sweat feeling on the left side of my neck which always indicates to me something is wrong. I don't know whereabouts on my body it is - all I know is that something is amiss. Obviously I thought it was the red area resurfacing but when Janet put me flat there was no sign that I'd aggravated it. I stayed flat until it was time for dinner but after sitting up for half an hour I again sensed something was wrong.

When Cary came on at eight I felt a bit grubby and she gave me a wash and changed my night shirt. It was then we discovered the reason why I had been uncomfortable. When the electric bed had put me into the sitting position, the overlaying Spenco mattress had nipped the left side of my lower back, leaving a raised red lump the size of a two pence piece. The Spenco is designed to be flexible and is stuffed in sections to give more protection - eleven days later after nursing the new mark by lying on a V cushion or sitting up with the cushion placed so it alleviated pressure, it gradually began to fade. The good news was the old posterior was fine!

So what did I do for eleven days? Well there were talking books, videos and Jack had sent me raffle tickets to sell for the parachute jump sponsorship. Then of course I had to fill in a disclaimer form and make an appointment with my doctor so he could confirm on the medical paper that I was fit to do a parachute jump! You didn't know that did you, Jack Berry?

I went to see my doctor a couple of days after I had spent a few hours back in the chair and even though I had been up most days to shower and wash my hair before returning to bed, my shoulders and neck ached with a vengeance. His only questions were, how and why. I told him, in tandem and to raise money for the IJF holiday. He sorted out a last minute hitch with the medical paper work, but I passed all health checks.

After using my electric chair for a normal ten-hour day in mid July I was pleased when I went to bed and had no red mark. That, however, didn't last long and I was back in my pushy chair after a week. The mark would go overnight but the area had obviously weakened. I decided just to use my pushy chair that wasn't marking me until after the parachute jump.

Before Janet, her husband Noel and myself drove up to Jack Berry's place in Cockerham, Lancashire, I appeared on Channel Four's Morning Line. Michelle and Janet had made me look as good as they could and I was really full of enthusiasm. I told the presenters that I would be skydiving from 10,000 feet - that's when they thought I had definitely lost it! I was going in tandem with a guy I had not met called Danny Smith of the Black Knights Parachute Centre and the aircraft that would take us above the clouds was an Islander light plane. They did not envy my task!

When we were on the M62, Noel suggested we stop somewhere for lunch, as we were in no hurry. I knew my mum would be at home and I like to surprise her so we made the diversion to Shipley. Janet was a little worried that she might not be in but she was. We had a lovely lunch and my uncle Michael joined us. I sold a few more raffle tickets in the pub and in the bookies!

I thought we would probably have an early night but by the time Jack and his wife Jo (who was an old weighing room colleague of mine) came home after racing it was quite late. The red wine was in my glass but I didn't over indulge myself. The one rule I have always adhered to is never to be inebriated before - a race ride - a scuba dive - or in this case a skydive!

In the morning I was interviewed by Gordon Brown for the Racing Channel, who were filming Jack's stables Open Day. I was upbeat, looking forward to my next fundraising stint. Afterwards we discussed the positioning of a camera that would be able to focus on my descent and Gordon wanted to capture my first reaction.

Jack's office had been inundated with 'Good Luck' messages from friends and acquaintances and I even received a 'phone call from Bill Shand-Kydd, who had already achieved this particular venture after breaking his neck in a team chase fall. He assured me it would be a wonderful experience - the thoughtfulness of people inspired me even more. It might not have been a Sheikh Mohammed horse but it was starting to feel like the next best thing!

I had already been told that it would be very cold as I plummeted from so high in the sky down towards the ground. This had been the main concern of Mr El Masry's when I asked him about my intended skydive. "So you're worried I'll get cold?" I queried. "Yes," he replied. "Not worried about the parachute opening then?!" Ironically the chill factor again. 'Déjà vu' or what? I would be prepared, I assured him.

I had already decided that underneath the supplied jump suit I would wear my sleeveless red Ferrari tee shirt, which I'd worn under my back protector when I was race riding. A light blue jumper with 'MURGY' emblazoned across the chest and Janet put my favourite tatty silk stock around my neck. "That should keep my neck warm," I joked with Janet "And stop the whiplash!" It felt right to wear my racing attire - I don't know why but it just did.

Janet and I arrived at the parachute club where we met my family and friends who had made a special effort to be with me. I met Danny Smith, the instructor I would be strapped to, who explained all procedures. We couldn't have asked for a more beautiful day and my mother had brought a lovely picnic. It was time for me to get into my skydiving jumpsuit. In order to do this I had to lie on a blanket in the aircraft hanger. Janet and one of the other instructors had to pull on the jumpsuit over my clothes. They had to roll me both ways making sure the harness was strapped on as tightly as I could possibly take it. It felt fine whilst I was horizontal but when Janet sat me up - I couldn't breathe - it was squashing my rib cage. The instructor loosened it off slightly and once I was sitting up in my wheelchair it all felt fine. The original time of 12.30pm had been changed to 2.30pm. Communications had been confused and that was the time I was pencilled in for.

To say I was disappointed when the rainstorm that we could see in the distance finally came thundering towards us is an understatement. I'd been sitting with the full kit on for three-and-a-half hours. Family and friends had made a special effort to be with me and that made it even worse. My poor school friend Lindsay Beanland smoked more fags in that time than we ever did at school! My mum was worried because Justine, my sister, was on her motorbike and all the people who had bought raffle tickets and were there on that day would be disappointed too. I felt that I'd let so many people down.

The rain hammered down on the light aircraft's hanger and there was no hiding my angst when Gordon Brown came to interview me again for The Racing Channel - instead of getting my first reactions after doing a skydive he filmed my disappointment although I vowed I would return at a re-scheduled time. I was amazed, when I returned home in the evening, that there were no red marks. After sitting around for all those hours in the harness I had felt sure I would be looking at days in bed again. The only consolation being that I would have done the parachute jump.

The new date for the skydive was 21st August which held a certain amount of significance as it was my niece Kelly's birthday. I played safe and only used my pushy chair beforehand. My mother was staying with me (suffering from a terrible summer cold) and we decided to drive up to Cockerham on the Sunday morning. It was an early start but Janet and I were used to that. We left at 5am and I just had a really good feeling as we drove north on what turned out to be a perfect day.

How can I describe what it is like to skydive? To begin with I went up with seven other guys so it felt a bit like the weighing room of old! Jack Berry decided he'd like a piece of the action so he sat up front with the pilot. The feeling of sheer freedom came after I was manoeuvred to the open door of the aircraft. My strapped-up limp legs hung over the edge of the plane as I, on Danny's third rock forward, was pushed out into the nothingness above the clouds. That's when pure exhilaration hit me - enhanced by my paralysed body as I couldn't feel that I was strapped to Danny. I was astonished at the spherical view below during the free fall for 5000 of the 10,000 ft descent. We plummeted back to terra firma at 120 mph - but it just felt like I was gliding on the airwaves.

Once the parachute was opened (it did work - and I wasn't cold...) I could have stayed up there all day. I experienced a bird's eye view and the rushing sound of free falling had now turned into serene calm with only the gentle fluttering of the parachute breaking through the silence, until Danny asked me if I was all right. He pointed out certain landmarks: Morecambe Bay, Jack Berry's stables - and the pub where he would be having a pint that night! After that I readily agreed to do a few somersaults and twirls. The ground did not come rushing up to meet us as we gently floated towards our landing mark. There were many hands ready to guide my legs to safety. One second I was airborne, the next I was lying in the grass on my side. There had been no awareness or sensation of impact - exactly the same feeling I had experienced before - and after - the last hurdle at Bangor. It was thrilling but it wasn't as adrenalin-seeking as I thought it would be. Those horses take some beating!

Jack invited all my supporters for the day (who included Johnny and Linda O'Hara, amongst family) back to his house where we celebrated with the customary champagne and Linda had bought me a silver brooch pin of a parachute. A couple of years later Johnny told me that he had felt 'most proud of me that day'. If only it had taken place on the original day when there had been so much publicity surrounding it, the Holiday Fund would have benefited by more than the £20,000 finally raised.

I had been red mark free for weeks and was pleased to be back in my electric chair and every night I hoped for whoever put me to bed to say "No marks - bottom's fine!"

It was early September when Gabriella, who had been my physio since returning home, rang me with the awful news that her daughter Joanna had suffered a stroke whilst on holiday in Spain. She was flying out immediately and didn't know when - or if - she would be able to resume my physio sessions. Even in her state of turmoil she told me to find an alternative physiotherapist so I could keep having my twice-weekly sessions of exercise that we both feel is vital.

I knew that Barbara Towler had two physios and rang to tell her of my predicament. One girl who treated her could come to me on a Tuesday morning and I said it would probably be temporary but as she had to travel from Peterbrough that arrangement was fine with her. Through Barbara's other physio I was put in touch with Lee Petrucci. I again relayed my situation to him and he could treat me for the two hours required on Fridays.

Lee is a sports physio and after a couple of sessions with him he asked me if I could lie on my front and the answer to that was yes. He thought I would benefit more if he treated me for an hour on a Thursday, massaging and loosening off my neck and shoulder muscles, then for an hour on Friday he could do more rotation work on my arms and neck. I agreed to this and did feel this new regime of exercising was better for me.

After six weeks of having my independence and thinking that I had finally seen the last of the red mark - it was back. It had gone by morning, but after my shower it was there again. The plastic shower chair was now also causing the area to break down.

By November I started to try out various cushions for my pushy chair and had ordered a new high level gel. After every clear week in that chair I'd go back in the mobile - sometimes for weeks, sometimes for days. I kept on skirting the issue but a change of cushions for both chairs looked imminent.

This was obviously now interfering with my social life and I had to decline a few supper dates with the girls. I knew my friend Alison Thom was working herself hard and I hadn't seen her for a while but when I rang and we chatted in late November there was no hint of how ill she was becoming. That would be the last time I would ever speak to my dear friend. Together with her husband, David, she had loyally supported me in my racing career. I didn't consider riding out with Ali to be work, we had fun, plenty of laughs and when a winner was ridden, we celebrated! She was released from the pain that had tormented her for longer than we knew on 11th December. Now those who were close to Ali had to learn to adjust to life without her.

Anna Ludlow read the following tribute I wrote for her - reflecting the sentiments of her closest friends.

Sleep Well

Sleep well now;
Now you are free
From all the pain and anguish
That sometimes we couldn't see.

Sleep well now;
Now the torment
Has left your heart and soul
Given you an angel's hand to hold.

Sleep well now;
Never to be afraid
Of the darkest night
Replaced now by celestial light.

Sleep well now
Alison
Sleep well.

So you can imagine as Christmas approached I was less than enthusiastic. This Christmas there would be no trivial arguments between my mum and me about the placing of decorations or whether the over-growing cheese plant should have white sticky backed baubles and silver tinsel placed on it. I spent most of my time in the office playing around with the computer and trying (most of the time) in vain to grasp more knowledge of how my year-old toy actually worked. The sound system was on its usual setting - high - keeping me oblivious to any activity that was taking place in the rest of the house.

My usual persistence at making the decisions as to what went where and reviewing the shopping list never materialised and I'd leave my mum to do what she wanted. Her concern that I never agree with what she does was often not even acknowledged.

The offer of food during these days was often refused - I didn't feel hungry. I was in my pushy chair more than the electric and had tried out a few different cushions, as I waited for the new high level gel. My original one was overdue for retirement. The disorder that was plain to see upset my mum but her fear that I was becoming anorexic was way off line. I was sitting about and not rushing around like her and the girls as they busied themselves with the hundred and one jobs that needed to be done in preparation for the festivities.

I was also concerned about my helper Shirley who had looked drawn and pale. She hadn't said anything to me but I knew something was wrong. I have a strong sense of knowing if anything is amiss with any of my ladies. Sometimes even hearing them in the kitchen or the way they walk down the hall alerts me to their mood. She was supposed to be going away with her partner for a Christmas break and had been looking forward to it. "All right for you, nipping off," I told her one morning as she was dressing me. That's when she told me her trip had been cancelled. She had split up with him and had been living with her daughter for the last week. Attempts for reconciliation were out of the question. So even though it was pretty gloomy all around, we still became embroiled in the hype as the end of the year approached.

Every New Year we reminisce about the disastrous time we decided to celebrate by self-catering in our Village Hall - where it had been freezing despite Nancy and husband Alan putting on all the heating in the afternoon. Only the faithful few turned up; I had a touch of fever and left a bottle of wine on the table at twenty to midnight - without any alcohol intake all evening everyone knew it was genuine!

Ever since then I've always had a small do at my house. This year would be no exception and we brought the New Year in with my brother Mark, Helen and a few friends. There were fireworks (my idea), the first barbecue of 2000 (Andy's idea) and the Millennium Prayer (mum's idea). Even in our small village fireworks were being let off in every direction. It was amazing to see the many blazes of colour and hear the fire-cracking sounds that shot into the still night. The systematic displays by the neighbourhood could not have made for better viewing. A few of my guests went out to the bottom of the drive and said there was a feeling that made the hairs on the back of their necks stand up - it was quite eerie.

My family all went back to Yorkshire and the girls and myself started to regain our usual back to work routine. Shirley was very unhappy and I hoped that things would soon sort themselves out. It was only four days into the New Year when her ex-partner was found dead. It was both tragic and shocking. Obviously she was devastated. In her turmoil her concerns about work were the last thing she should even be thinking of I stressed. Without hesitation, the rest of the girls rallied round to cover all her duties. She had our full support and nothing was too much trouble for anyone. Bravely, she returned to work three weeks later.

My weekend-long birthday celebration in February came to an end at about 8pm but after being in my electric chair all day the pressure had again left a red mark. My hope was fading that I would heal and be back to normal. It became increasingly obvious that I would need a pressure-relieving cushion for my electric chair - still I was reluctant to change.

Over the next few months I tried many cushions and the patience of many salesmen! A sale was all they were interested in - do I look stupid? Their wonderful product could do anything bar take me to the moon - and fit properly into my electric chair. On one occasion I was perched up on an 'all air-circulating, singing and dancing pumped-up bottom saver, a mere steal at £850'. A blind man could have seen I was only just managing to keep my balance. My arms propped me up by leaning on the arm rests with shoulders under ears, looking stiff and rigid and hoping nobody exhaled without warning or they would have seen me topple out side ways - and this guy said with a wide grin:

"Good isn't it - can you feel the slight movement of the continuous airflow?"

"Er, no, but you'll see the very fast movement of me hitting the floor in about ten seconds!"

I decided to stay in my pushy chair until I got sorted out. I was still trying to master my computer and the positioning of the chair was crucial for my comfort. So all in all, an often good day was followed by a couple of bad ones, not least for me but Shirley as well.

We were all ready for a holiday by the time it came round and once again it was most enjoyable. I was very careful and there was only the odd trace of a red mark. It held up well during the holiday.

Unfortunately the 'plane journey home aggravated it and the customary few days in bed followed. I wanted to be in good order to attend Newmarket races on 2000 Guineas day.

It was beautiful weather for the May meeting and I decided to wear a pale lilac dress suit. The sleeveless dress with a mandarin collar and slight print enhanced my suntan - I felt nice. Romney, my publishers, had a stand selling my books (amongst others) and, after watching the Queen officially opening the new Millennium Stand, I went to sign a few of them. My mum and Shirley took me and we met Michelle at the bookstall.

The wheelchair stand was full by the time we got there so we watched the first race down on the grass about six deep off the rails - well…watch is not really true - not in my case. I could just about hear the thunder of hooves going past the winning post amidst the massive shouting crowd that made the commentary inaudible. We all looked at each other, none the wiser as to who had won. One place for me to make a mental note of - never go there again!

My eagerness to make racing enjoyable for everyone who accompanies me (mainly not racing people now) is sometimes a difficult one. I knew that the racecourse would be packed but that is my whole point of going racing on such a day - to see the really good horses in the flesh and hope that the passion I feel about the sport will reach the others - unfortunately you either have it or you don't.

To compensate I said I'd buy them all a drink. Unbeknown to me what had formerly been the Owners' and Trainers' bar (equipped with ramp) that had allowed me in with my jockey's badge, was now only for Annual Members. Michelle and Shirley went for the drinks elsewhere whilst mum and I waited in the shade. I had a chance to say hello to many racing acquaintances - for whom it seemed the bar was still in use!

My view for the big race was essential otherwise I might as well have watched it in the comfort of my own home. We headed for the new Millennium Stand in plenty of time to secure a place in the designated disabled area. Going up in the lift was brilliant, the view over the paddock was fantastic - I could have stayed in there if I'd been able to see the race!

The lift opened to reveal a throng of people. Our requests of "Excuse me" were met by "Sorry love," or "Move out of the way mate, let the ladies through". When we reached the doors that would take us out to the grandstand, a young girl security officer pointed out the wheelchair area. "If there is anybody in there just ask them to move," she told us. We somehow managed to manoeuvre through the crowd only to find the wheelchair stand was packed - with able-bodied people, mostly men but also quite a few women. As soon as our "excuse me" was heard, everyone willingly moved to let me secure my rightful viewing place. Everyone -

except two women in their late 40s or early 50s. An unpleasant exchange of words ensued.

The two women were standing in the right hand corner of the stand. Michelle tapped one of them on the arm, asking them politely if they could let me in the corner. I have to sit at a right angle as my right side took the brunt of damage when I hit the deck; the neck-breaking fall left me with restricted head mobility when looking right - even after years of physiotherapy - but the left side has responded beyond expectation.

Both women looked round and I smiled as they half-heartedly shuffled along a few steps, mumbling to each other. They still didn't leave enough room for me to squeeze in. My footplates were up against the Perspex that covered the bottom half of the stand. Once again Michelle tapped the bespectacled one asking for a little more room.

"We've been here all day," she barked.

"Well, this is the disabled stand," Michelle pointed out.

"Where does it say that?" she asked.

Another woman with a small child had already moved for us and confirmed that it was. By this time my mum and Shirley were out of earshot. I still couldn't see properly and as Michelle tried to angle me, the woman, now quite indignant, enquired:

"How much room do you want?" She directed the question straight at me. Not a very good question in the circumstances, was it? All I'd done was smile and say thanks.

"Just enough room so I can see, please." I was calm - an angry scene was something I didn't want to happen in front of my mum. I could see right down the track but as they muttered, leaning forward over the top rail, there was no way I'd be able to see the closing stages. Thinking I would defuse the tension I then tapped the woman on the arm and asked her if she could stand straight during the closing stages - showing her that if I leant forward - we could both see the last furlong. You could say that's when things became unpleasant.

"Is there anything else you'd like me to do?" Her voice was heavy with sarcasm.

Two men who were standing on the next step down from the stand told the woman to 'leave it' but she was on a roll and continued:

"I am a Member, you know." I butted in, "So am…" "If you'll let me finish; wouldn't you be better off down there?" She pointed down towards the rails - where I had been earlier.

They were off for the 2000 Guineas; I watched the later stages on the big screen after making a point of leaning forward. Thankfully the ignorance of these two women had been directed at me and not at a newly injured person still coping with their different situation - still only being able to see the barriers and the things they cannot do any more. Even when it feels like one is being overlooked - never let anybody break the spirit that is you.

By the end of the month it was time for my MOT (every other year) at Oswestry with Mr El Masry. I am always keen to go as I make a night of it and see the rugby boys. I particularly wanted to speak to him about my ongoing pressure problem. As always, he was very concerned but felt I was doing everything I could - "It's basically pressure and the only way to alleviate it is to keep off it."

Apart from that blip I was in good order. I was surprised, after being weighed, to find I was only 8 stone 9 lbs; I'd lost 1 stone 5 lbs since that horrendous day in Newmarket when I weighed in at 10 stone. The only thing was I didn't feel as if I had.

Sean Evans had been notified by Vicky Jones in advance (as usual) that we were staying the night and, as far as I knew, only Robin, Jan, Alex and Platty would be there. I was taken aback when Trev and Frank appeared to help me out of the car. They had both been out of the country and although Frank had returned for only one week he fitted me in for a drink between his Auntie and his Granny! Trev ate with us but had to leave early due to a prior engagement. After all these years I was touched that they still made time for me.

Within a few days I was dismayed to find, yet again, my red mark was back and that was in my pushy chair - with the new gel cushion. I also felt a bit jaded so the next few days in bed were welcome although I still got up for a shower (wrapping a towel round the seat until a padded cushion could be organised, ordered and arrive) and physio. The plus side was that Royal Ascot was on - so uninterrupted telly viewing there! However, it was becoming increasingly obvious that I would definitely need a new electric chair - I was like a flaming yo-yo for the rest of the summer…

As soon as I felt better I assured Serena that after trying a few more options with the Tec 50, I would look at other chairs. The upshot of my idea to take the fixed padded seat off the Tec 50 and replace it with a gel cushion was a long drawn-out procedure that seemed to work - for one day. I even tried two gels - still no good. So it was back to lying flat until I could sit up in bed for a reasonable amount of time.

Don't feel sorry for me, Wimbledon was on! My only disappointment being that Goran Ivanisevic was knocked out in an early round. He came on the scene in the early 90s and I've been through all those agonising semis and finals with him ever since. So you can imagine how delighted I was this year. Now there's a man with passion in his soul!

Enter Colin from Cambridge Mobility. We have known each other for quite a few years as he services wheelchairs - so no salesman talk there - and no, he doesn't think I look stupid! Colin brought round the first of many electric chairs but I didn't try it straight away. The reason was that I had been asked months before if I would be Guest of Honour at the Portland College's Award Day and had accepted. I said to Janet that I really must go even if it set me back a bit. I'd been in bed for such long periods that I was in a dilemma over whether my mark would have subsided sufficiently for me to take the chance. I was still feeling awful about not attending Arthur Jones' funeral, this being the family that had almost put their life on hold whilst I was recovering in Oswestry. I had agonised over making the trip, until Vicky Jones rang me and said, "Father would understand, Sharron." It didn't make me feel vindicated - and I hoped I wouldn't have to let anyone else down.

The Portland College in Nottingham is a fantastic place where kids and adults can learn different skills. Many of the younger award winners were severely disabled from birth but had still managed to achieve something and the pleasure on their faces was moving to say the least. I thought of Arthur - they would have impressed him - as they did me.

I tried Colin's silver dream machine - I think not... After two hours with my gel cushion I sensed something was wrong, as I became clammy around my neck. Janet put me back on the bed and, when she looked, there was an angry, raised, red area - not funny.

Unbelievably, once again I dropped in lucky - the Olympics! Gee Armytage, aware of my ongoing situation, telephoned me. "You poor thing, you must be so bored." "You are joking, aren't you, Gee? The Olympics are on!" I had even become quite nocturnal. I can remember where I was when Steve Redgrave won his fifth gold medal! I had urged the boys on but had to do it quietly so as not to wake my sleeping ladies. Earlier in the summer when I was on one of my enforced periods of bedrest, Gee and boyfriend Mark came to visit and she had enquired then about boredom. I relayed a number of various interests that kept boredom at bay:

Sky News, World News, documentaries, films, talking books, David Bowie videos, Eddie Izzard video, Alan Davis video (I love comedy) - she stopped me there. "And of course Andy and Keith often pop in. Did I mention David Bowie videos?" "Yes!"

One evening Joss 'phoned and I told her, "I'm in bed - finding myself!"

"Oh, couldn't you afford the fare to Egypt?" "No, I didn't want to go in De nial." Big laugh!

The downside of lounging around in bed is that when I start sitting up it has to be for a few hours at a time, gradually staying up for longer periods. It disrupts life in general and you can't make plans to do anything because you just have to take it day by day. It is also a lot of hassle for my ladies who get me up and dressed only to put me back in bed. The pressure on my neck and shoulders makes them ache relentlessly and all in all, it is a bloody nuisance.

There were occasions when I would just lie and think about different times, experiences and my life; one being my 1995 holiday from hell in Dubai! Bryn Crossley suggested I go there for a week in the sun. I decided I would, and accompanied by Janet and Joan I flew off on a cold December morning. We arrived on a rainy December afternoon - the rain would last for a week except for two hours on the Thursday afternoon. Forever imprinted on my mind will be the hour and a half I spent in the Persian Gulf. I insisted on being left with the waves softly lapping over my front wheels even though they were ever so slightly digging into the sand. I had seen two sunbeds about 20 metres away and suggested to Janet and Joan that they go and relax - enjoy this so far elusive sun. The sand and sea spread out as far as the eye could see and there was not another soul in sight. Magic.

I contentedly enjoyed the serenity, then out of the corner of my eye I saw what seemed to be a rather good-looking man walking towards me. I deduced he wasn't a local. With sunglasses, book in hand and towel slung over his shoulder I felt a greeting was surely imminent. There was nobody else around (excuse me). How could he possibly walk past without saying a word? When he was about seven metres away I prepared myself for conversation, then, as soon as he was within earshot, my two minders popped up behind me to ensure my front wheels were not sinking into the sand as the waves retreated.

"Are you okay?" He said, "Hi" and was gone, to which I exclaimed; "You've just stopped me pulling on the Persian Gulf!"

Back to reality. A variety of electric chairs were brought round which I had picked out of the brochure but I could tell, just by looking, that some of them would be no good. Again, they could do anything you wanted and in any colour, but they were big and cumbersome. However, the Tec 50, whilst being a fairly big chair, looked neat and I sat into it more - I didn't need the high-tech big models with all their extras. All these others seemed to shout 'big wheelchair coming' and a lot of people might think - so what, what's wrong with that? My personal preference is that you see the person - not the disability.

When I EVENTUALLY got to staying up all day it was in my push-around chair while I waited for the new chair. For a fortnight I had a trial chair and, after testing it with a soft back, hard back, tilt back, I was finally pleased I had found that the hard-backed version suited me.

So once again I'd had a taste of my independence and now I had to wait for delivery. I was becoming quite adept on my computer - it had to come sooner or later! So when Andy told me he was building a web page advertising his business, I became really enthusiastic and he helped me to do one of my own. We copied and pasted two photos, one of me on a horse before the start of a race and the other was the photo of me feeding 'Fiefdom' a mint that had been on the front cover of *Jump Jockeys Don't Cry*. I could write whatever I liked and e-mail the address to any of my friends and we could have two links on the page. He was one of mine and vice versa. I've got a good title for the page, I told him. "What's that?" "On the other side of the fence."

In late November the chair arrived. It wasn't exactly right but Shirley managed to alter my desk and after all the fuss of the past year I took delivery of a Tec 45 (one model down from the original!) - not as fast but likes the bottom!

One River

In my corner of time
Where for me the living is fine
With light and dark
Day and night and half night.
Following a path with many places to go
Destined to live my life – taking on every fight.

All these things I know
And I can see my river that flows.
If only you could see me
Like you did before
Then one river could flow.

Wandered out on a summer's day
Breeze ruffling up my hair.
Playing, dancing, over land
Sunlight glowing through drifting clouds,
I reach out for a hand
Only to find
There are many shadows - reflecting on the sand.

All these things I know
And I can see a river that flows.
If only they could see you
Like they did before
Then your river could flow.

Slept through a night that was warm
In my corner of time
I knew I had it all.
You and I sailed down a stream
Only to find
This was another day – not another dream.

All these things I know
And I can see the river that flows.
If only they could see us
Like they did before
Then one river could flow.

CHAPTER TEN

WHAT IT FEELS LIKE FOR THIS GIRL

I look at the reflection in the mirror and sometimes don't recognise the person who looks back, not least because the ageing process has started, even though I feel as if I've been in a time warp. The all-important body image is sometimes okay - mostly not okay. The slackening of stomach muscles, relentless in their progress, makes me feel ugly. I face this demon every day but my immobilised state renders me powerless to conquer it - however much I try.

The constant reliance on others to perform the most personal tasks of a dysfunctional body is a realisation of how vulnerable one has become. There are the many things that are taken for granted: the simplicity of running a hand through my hair or frustration at watching others busy themselves by setting a table and making dinner; the luxury of soaking in a bubble bath, snuggling between crisp fresh sheets and being enveloped by a hugging duvet is a distant dream - as is the feeling of ground beneath bare feet. When the stretching of arms to give or receive a hug - is awkward. I've striven to keep my femininity amidst the perception of being 'one of the boys'. A part of me revels in this and yet at the same time - I look at them knowing they see me through blind men's eyes...

My ambition that drove me on to the point of greed in the late 80s - grasping every opportunity I could with both hands - came under heavy criticism from friends and family (overtime again - with raised eyebrows) that hurt. I strove to put in the work of two people only to find there weren't enough hours in the day for me to work and ride another horse. Why? Because 'you reap what you sow' apparently. I look out now at the sun and blue sky pouring its goodness on the carpet of green grass and it seems to beckon to me. I often yearn to get up and go and sometimes it's easier to deal with the physical pain and reverberations of a late night than feel bright, breezy, pain free and alive. My beloved horses that I had lived and breathed for are gone now - leaving me with the memory of their touch, odour, idiosyncrasies and power-filled gallop. That may fade with time but will never be extinguished.

A romantic at heart - one of the greatest things we can experience is to love and be loved in return, when the passion and obsession takes precedence, letting heart rule the head. Then realising the very thing you always wanted slid away - without a second glance. So you try to fill one part of passion with another. But that knotted feeling in the pit of your stomach still manages to send a message (even through a broken body) to your brain when you hear the words of your favourite love songs, reminding you that you are not dead inside...

The times when not conforming are deemed as awkward only because of the wheelchair, not because I have a different opinion; and apparently any change of mood is because of the wheels and lots of people think I cannot speak because I'm permanently sitting down!

Multiply those few points by forever - and some people will still barely understand what I'm talking about.

The bravado of my sport has given me the courage to live with the debilitating changes in my life. I know how lucky I am - I know there are many people who have never experienced the high euphoria of riding a winner or the gift of being loved. I know there are many much worse off than me. I made my own choices and I can live with them. Truth and Fact.

I was emotionally drained at the time of my fall and I resigned myself to a life alone as soon as I knew I would be wheelchair-bound. This was what I felt was right for me. It was easy to keep the emotional door closed to men and many other issues. I took on - no I didn't take it on, it was an already built-in instinct (maybe for my own survival) to be 'The Rock that feels no pain' and 'The Island that never cries'. It wasn't artificial and it certainly wasn't contrived but in doing so I have used my wheelchair and effectively created a barrier. The self-preservation often used by jockeys kicking in at last!

This has given out two very different messages. The aforementioned 'being one of the boys' and then this bizarre idea that my easiness in the company of men (who often don't really know me) has been misconstrued, by them, not to see me because I may fall in love with them!

Please!

I am perceived by some as being 'brave' - fair comment; 'hard' - ouch; 'brusque' - sometimes; 'unapproachable' - I didn't think so; 'obnoxious and loud' - that's the drink talking! Anything else? 'Sarcastic' - my attempt at humour? 'Bossy' - well, I'd do it myself but for obvious reasons...; 'Lady Muck' - didn't see that one coming! 'Queen of Sheba' and, apparently, I come from 'Planet Murgatroyd' - I thought I was quite sweet! There are many ways to describe me but apparently 'sweet' isn't one of them!

So how does a once private individual capable of doing a variety of jobs, involving the running of a house, working in a highly charged business where mistakes are crucial and being rollicked is all part of the territory - as are insult and injury - react?

I know who and what I am and I'm sorry if I offend. I don't mean to.

On my own insistence, as soon as I had established a team of ladies I wanted to be independent even from my close friends. I didn't want to impose myself upon them. They had already been a tremendous support and I of all people know how racing engulfs your time.

My life and that of my friends had already started to go in different directions, naturally everybody was moving on. For instance my great friend, Joss, moved north to the Highlands of Scotland (but she is back now) and Lucie Hide had become Mrs Woods by marrying Sean. I was invited to the wedding accompanied by Richard Phillips, which was also attended by my ex-fiancé, with whom I had severed all contact shortly after my return home from Oswestry. The gulf of silence between us could last forever but the respect I felt we both deserved would allow us to acknowledge each other, from a distance of course, on this our friends' special day. Despite the wet weather, in the company of my friends Jenny and Bruce Raymond, Jeff and Lydia Pearce, in true racing fashion we partied late into the night.

I was also growing as a person and had to carve out a new life for myself - which probably, and in the end, didn't involve my friends directly. When we did meet up it was to reminisce and have a laugh. I didn't want anyone to feel sorry for me. In fact sometimes I'd see a forlorn look and know I was the cause of it.

Dreams are always so real, hence the poem at the beginning of the book, which captivated me. My vivid dreams are a mixture of the past and present. For the first few years I was sometimes in a wheelchair but now I am always walking, often riding and racing. I've written many poems or prose based on an entire dream. Often when a bout of insomnia invades my sleeping hours I can get a title out of the air as I lie mulling things over contentedly. Other times I resort to television - yes, I am a channel hopper - all 157 of them and nothing worth watching!

My fortieth birthday passed without any ill feeling. I couldn't think what all the fuss was about regarding this milestone in life, despite the fact that for most of the year I was still nursing my red mark.

Then all of a sudden towards the end of the year all hell broke loose (within myself). Everything I did seemed to be scrutinised, criticised or laughed at. I felt my requests were met argumentatively. My confidence slumped to an all time low and I felt worthless. I was on the edge of an abyss - the very thing that could never happen to me was starting to fester.

I felt like a time bomb waiting to go off and everyone seemed to be closing in on me. I was fed up with silly jokes sent via email and all the banter with Keith was just winding me up - he was right when he said I'd had a sense of humour failure! One day it was unfortunate for Keith, but contrived by me, that a usual quip from him when I was feeling particularly hostile, saw me blast out a volley of expletives. He took the full brunt of my frustration and anger at feeling useless - he was the only one who could take it and not be offended. He was oblivious as to what I had been going through and can't recall the incident.

Maybe ten years of unintentionally suppressing my emotions was even too much for this hardy old 'rock that feels no pain and island that never cries'. So many questions without answers, or was the answer so simple I missed it? This had nothing to do with the wheelchair and the debilitating fall. I have often stressed I would not exchange my life with anybody else. This was about me and what a million other men and women go through at different times in their life. Justification.

I might not be able to control every aspect of my life but I can have total control of what is in my head. I was in a rut - looking back through rose coloured glasses instead of looking forward to the new horizons I so often practice and preach about. I know what it feels like to be loved and I will never live through that emotional pain of rejection again - that pain which feels like you are lying naked in the snow. But the one thing I had not resigned myself to was complete closure.

I retreated for a while (a few days) and lost myself in my much loved music. I wanted someone to walk into my life and out of my dreams... This was not going to happen and I berated myself: "No - sort yourself out, pull yourself together, get a life, basically, get off your backside and find something to do - like you always have done. Make things happen!"

By Christmas 2000 I had started writing this book.

Now, I realise I am normal after all - the last two years of emotional trauma that had surrounded me, as well as my own misgivings and unhappiness at doing nothing, had caught up with me... Fantastic! I am human. I do not come from Planet Murgatroyd (contrary to rumour), I do not come with framework, wheels, pump and instructions of how to assemble in three easy steps permanently stuck to my forehead! Well, to be fair, I have had a ten-year cooling-off period!

While I am busy writing, my only needs are drink and loo breaks. I love to have my music on loud when working alone, a trait not shared by all. There are always the usual daily chores for the girls to do and I feel I'm in the best place!

Unfortunately, Nancy 'cook me something' had not been feeling very well for a few weeks and as she is Social Services input they rang to say she was on sick leave as from that day. Nancy has been cooking for me since 1992 which is marvellous because there are times when I'm on the 'phone and she simply presents a culinary delight for that evening's meal. She lives in the village so, unfortunately for her, if I need any assistance at odd times of the day I know I can always SOS her. We (the other girls) rallied round although there wasn't much we could do but she knew how worried we were about her. In her own words she 'lost the plot for a while' but swears it was nothing to do with working here! Luckily for me she is back in full working order.

When the annual Injured Jockeys' Fund holiday came round you could say I was less than enthusiastic. Michelle packed my cases while I stayed transfixed to my computer screen, with the odd 'yes', 'no' or 'I don't know' to any enquiries about clothes, jewellery or shoes. The music forever pounding. Some days I'd get a real run on with the writing and then all of a sudden it would be 6pm - Nancy would arrive to make my dinner and I'd manage to squeeze in another few minutes. I knew my right shoulder couldn't take the pace but the physical pain was part of the job. 'If you're going to moan about it - don't do it'!

For all my imperfections (of which there are many) and especially while I've been writing this book - there were times when I've been quite terse with a few people! My hours at the computer hardly produce enough work for any rate of pay. If I had been on piecework - I'd be minus nothing! A frustrating two days of 'not a lot' followed up my elation of typing 1000 words one day. I'd given myself a deadline and it had to be met to restore my self-esteem and it became imperative that I did it without seeking advice or reassurance. It will take a while for all feelings of self-deprivation to be swept away and as I write, I still feel the need to pressurise myself to achieve more. I knew I wouldn't be able to take any criticism, however constructive it may be. Not until I had finished. I was almost secretive - I needed to do the 110% - the all or nothing... Truth and Fact.

So for me it was great to have my good friend Joss help me with the typing. I dictated, and her expert keyboard skills just about managed to keep up when I was in good voice! We have been through many high and low times together and our friendship is solid. Even so, I still felt the need to type as much as I could without her.

I asked Michelle if she would spring clean Becklyn, while I was on the annual Tenerife holiday. The place needed a good going over. She offered to give it a lick of paint as well and I gave her a free hand. There were many items that had to be changed - some were more than ten years past their sell by date!

Nevertheless, it is hard to let go of the many entities that you gather along this path of life; be it material or otherwise. The changing over is slow - sometimes humorous because what you perceive as still worthy of its place is regarded by others, who are only trying to help, as junk. Keeping your own identity in your own home is important but many items have to be replaced, either perished or outdated; the new objects, even if I've chosen them, can somehow never measure up to their predecessors. When you look at them with a smile remembering where they came from and who had given that particular gift. How you had handled and polished them with the very same hands that can now no longer hold or feel anymore - the sentimental value forever holding the highest price - well, in my case anyway...

I was ready and grateful for ten days in the sun by the time it came round. But I wasn't ready for the emotional effect it would have on me. If I thought nothing could ever touch my shielded heart then I was wrong, even though the young age of so many injured people had always upset me.

I'd met Scott Taylor at the Lesters with his carer, Teresa, a month before the holiday. Scott, a tough northern jockey, had kicked home 56 winners as well as being an ex-boxing champion. I'd seen his fall on the television and it looked a cruncher - it was. The Perth ground was unforgiving on 20th August 1999 and left him with a severe head injury where both mobility and speech were badly affected. His heart stopped whilst in the ambulance and he was resuscitated on the way to the Ninewells hospital in Dundee. He was 27. His affinity with the Maurice Barnes-trained front-running Caulker was well known by northern racegoers.

It must be frustrating, painful and infuriating to know exactly what is going on - what is being asked or said - but be unable to release the voice that cries out in your head so clearly the words you want to say...

By contrast, the 26-and (most important) a-half year old Shane Broderick who on first sight I felt empathy with - had plenty of voice! I clearly remember taking a special interest as I saw the Irish horse 'Doran's Pride' being backed for the Stayers' Hurdle at the Cheltenham Festival in 1995. Connections obviously thought this kid was good (a boy in a man's world) and he steered 'Doran's Pride' round the undulating contours of Cheltenham to win. They returned two years later on 13th March and finished third in the Gold Cup. On the last day of the same month he lay on the Fairyhouse turf fighting for his life after a neck-breaking fall - he was 22 years old. Another spinal injury: he was left with a little shoulder movement...

Shane was a modest, unassuming Irish jockey who had touched the big time with 'Doran's Pride'. "Not as flamboyant as colleague Paul Carberry," recalls former ace Irish amateur, now racecourse commentator and Grand National winning trainer, Ted Walsh. He followed this up with, "He was a boy who rode with a cool head and confidence - more in the Dunwoody/Bradley mould." That made me wonder if it was harder to cope with the loss of limbs when you know that you were good - or does he feel privileged to have felt that overwhelming euphoria?

It isn't - and he does, are the answers to those. He was neither bitter nor angry at his destiny. "There's nothing we can do about it, so we've just got to get on with it - haven't we?"

"Yes," I replied.

Still, I often caught a confused and longing look in both the boys' faces - when something triggers a past memory that reminds you of what life used to be like before. It took me back to my days in hospital where I shared a ward with a bunch of kids with broken necks - never to recover and resume normal life. It tears at me to see these kids and I think why them - why them?

I know everyone found it hard to say goodbye at the end of that holiday even though we'd had the usual banter and laughter, plus for the last two years our own in-house comic, Richard Fox. 'Foxy', a former top lightweight jockey is not only very witty but also has a deep caring side that is more often than not overlooked - and he says that I am quite sweet. However, this last holiday had seemed so different to any other, for me anyway - I know I'm getting old - I decided to keep my sunglasses firmly on and so did most of the others. When we went down to see Shane, Martin and Vincent (who I'd nicknamed 'Starry, Starry Night' for obvious reasons) off for their journey home, the outside of the complex seemed to be charged with emotion. I said goodbye to Shane and told him that next year he will have to heed my advice of 'pacing himself'!

I found it amazingly easy to resume working on the book when I returned home even though it had upset me to see how Shane had had his active young life cut so drastically short. I could understand now how my mum has felt for the duration of these past years - when she willingly would have taken the physical pain away if she could.

A few sleepless nights on holiday had alerted me to address many more issues in depth for this book. So when the good weather came round I kept saying no to invitations out. I enforced a daily grind of writing upon myself. Interruptions started to drive me demented. I was working - all I wanted to do was write - I needed to push myself to the edge. I had to regain my strength and sense of purpose. Even physio was starting to get in the way (and I did cancel a few appointments) but without it, I feared the right shoulder would have had to be amputated! At least my arms could move and they were in pain for a reason. That's good pain.

I have taken the liberty to be my own redeemer. It is not fair to put that burden on anyone else. My determination to ride horses and ride winners will always be a part of me. When the frivolity or bravado of another day slips away with the light - leaving me arranged and alone for the night - passion and love will always be a part of me. Resting peacefully as I treasure my solitude. Truth.

Life is different now but it still must not be wasted - perversely, I look back on my life when I was mobile and realise how much more I could have done to enhance it and help others who I shared it with. I've been a little naïve, I feel. For instance, I now know about body language - language, fluent - body; well I've a small problem there now. Ah yes, it's quite noticeable isn't it?

Dreamer

Dreamer; You come to me
Now you're part of my life.
With strong arms you lift me from my bed
So I can stand on my tiptoes.
Kiss your neck as you hold me close
With wanton passion we both know
Whispering, please don't let me go.
For we can dance and play and tease
Before the morning light
When you need to take me.

Dreamer; I wait in another night
Knowing you will be with me soon
You gently lift and kiss my palm
Hold it against your beating heart;
Rock me slowly to and fro
A warm embrace to play your part.
Then you look deep into my eyes
Those feelings we can never disguise.
Whispering please don't let go
Hold me forever in dark of night,
Let the hours crawl by like years
No place now for anyone's tears.

Dreamer; I know you came to part my life
I leave my hand for you to hold
I feel you rest your head upon my breast,
Hoping to hear the soft slow beat
But no sound is there
For I'm not alive when I'm asleep.
I cannot waken
I am the life you have forsaken
Whispering please don't let me go.
My eyes stay closed, you want them to
For you cannot look at me
Nor I at you.

CHAPTER ELEVEN

AUGUST 2nd 2001

As I approach the 10th year since 'My Last Fling', I can hardly believe it...

That turned out to be one hell of a ride!

I have changed immensely over the last ten years and even while I've been writing this book! The mayhem and magic of my life have kept me on a vital learning and living curve.

A man wrote to me in April of this year. He couldn't remember who said it, but someone described 'our length of stay on earth as being just for a weekend' and after reading *Jump Jockeys* he deduced that I'd had a fantastic Saturday and felt that I would have a wonderful Sunday. I don't know if Sunday has started yet but as I look back, evaluating my past, I think how lucky I've been. That first time I pulled the colours on to ride 'Jolliffes Double' and walked towards the parade ring alongside my good friend Lydia Pearce will never be traded. The sheer elation I felt when I was legged up to ride the same horse a number of years later at Cheltenham - but then the mortification that came after being unseated at the fifth, which led to his sad demise.

My attraction towards quotes started when I was seventeen and read: 'The boldest and most ridiculous hope - has sometimes been the cause of extraordinary success'. I aspired to these words and wrote them on the back of a picture of a horse I was looking after. At times I was 'the boldest' and did have 'the most ridiculous hope'. Those words put me in the saddle that day and that is why I am in this seat today. I feel the work is not over for those words as they still have a relevant part to play in my life. I would like to do many different things - broadening my horizons cannot stop now - if ever!

My love of music has hardly gone unnoticed in this book and if only I wasn't tone deaf in voice, maybe I could have cut a demo tape singing my own lyrics - the mixture of words and music has helped me to achieve a multitude of tasks. I cut off outside interference by surrounding myself with music. My tunnel vision kicks in (some things can never change), I'm quiet - but Bowie is very loud.

Apparently music stimulates creativity in the brain; it is also said that left-handed people are more creative than right-handed. I was right-handed, loved loud music and wrote a few poems before the fall - so now

I have all the right attributes, as my left arm has to do 98% of all my work so there shouldn't be anything good left out!

I am totally moved by people who are passionate about their sport. I feel I can identify with every frustrated expletive - I've been there and when it is all in front of you ready for the taking, you have to grab it - tomorrow isn't promised. I see many, often young people, who don't seem to have any enthusiasm for life and I want to shake them and say, "There is so much out there, so much to see and do. Don't waste your life and limbs on pettiness. Open your eyes and ears - you don't need money to do everything - there are many things you just can't buy!"

So now to the people in my life. I have already addressed my loving family and the rugby boys - but there are my loyal and mainstay close friends that I'll have for all time. Joss Drake, who has helped with the typing of this book when my arms and shoulders have cried enough - even though she has suffered a constant battle with her own health since she was fourteen. Our friendship is one where we can be at all times brutally honest with each other.

Jennie Raymond (Jen) who became not only my 'best going-racing buddy' but was a great friend indeed when I returned home with a wheelchair instead of a saddle. She helped sort out my finances and we shared many bottles of red wine! We were part of Team GB with Amanda Perrett, née Harwood, Carolyn Eddery, Jo Winter and Elaine Bronson in 1989 for the ladies international race and hammered those European girls when they took us on at York!

Alison Thom (Ali), so instrumental in getting me settled back in my own home. I think about you often 'girlie', telling me I used to ride my two-year-old filly 'And Me' too short and I'd say nothing just in case I hit the deck and when the day came that I did, I was riding long as we were only trotting! Save me a space next to you on that cloud - and for God's sake make sure it has wheelchair access...

I am so pleased that I could help my old mate Lydia Pearce (LP) out when a car accident ended in a fatality and consequently her husband was jailed. She was my friend no matter what and it's a good feeling for me to be here for her - even though the circumstances are dreadful. She won the Ladies Championship five times during the 90s - only because I wasn't fit to ride, I tell her, and she knows how lucky she has been as I let delusions of grandeur creep into my head. It doesn't seem that long ago (1978) when we were stable girls at Jeremy Hindley's Clarehaven stables both holding the burning ambition to race ride - both agreeing that our role model was Elain Mellor, for her verve and professionalism in flat racing.

This seven times Champion Lady Jockey still holds the record. She always had time to help and taught me how to pull my goggles down, by placing a thumb underneath the elastic, pulling them over the peak of the colour cap, over my eyes, then letting the thumb slip the elastic into place at the back of my helmet. One smooth movement - the right way - the professional way.

It would be unforgivable of me to leave out my long gone racing rivals on the track and buddies. The irrepressible Elaine Bronson who rings me at least three times a year from Australia and always manages to find a lift to Newmarket when she comes back to England.

Lorna Vincent, the woman who gave us hope and inspiration to emulate her as lady jump jockeys, rings me and on one occasion had a favour to ask that I had a word with her friend who had read *Jump Jockeys Don't Cry* and was going through a rough patch. The friend in question was Julie Krone, America's most prolific winning lady rider! Candy and Billy Morris always greet me with open arms - not afraid to hug...

John Francome's laddish behaviour is going to be blown away now! He is a thoughtful and compassionate man - only the lucky few witness this side of him. Together with Jim McGrath (who cannot keep a secret), I have two very different sounding boards. Jim is a kind and supportive man and I can talk over more serious matters with him, yet at the same time he is also very humorous and tells me I'm bossy! Their off-the-cuff phone calls to enquire how I am are often funny and sometimes lewd (that definitely is them not me). To hear them regaling a story about each other is hilarious but once I start telling them a long drawn out story of what I've been up to - suddenly Jim's other line starts ringing and Francome's "Got to go, there's someone at the door!" My time is up - but how fortunate I am. Truth and Fact.

My journey goes on and I have met many new faces and also been in touch with a couple of very old ones. Namely two guys I knew 27 years ago, when I was a teenager! My school friend Lindsay Beanland and I have kept in touch and I told her I was going to delve into my past, but not in a million years did I ever think I'd be going this far! Nigel Long wrote to me after he had read *Jump Jockeys*. He broke his neck playing rugby in his early twenties and was left with much the same mobility as myself. Through him and the powers of e-mail I'm now in contact with the other name from my past - Chris Wood, living in Thailand. 'I don't believe it' or 'you cannot be serious' - come to mind.

As many of my racing colleagues, male and female, retire, I feel a small sense of loss. I no longer see their names in the paper, unless of course they take up training or stay in racing and just relocate out of the weighing room area. Now their time in the saddle is over and I hope like me they enjoyed the rollercoasting ride.

The setting up of JETS - 'Jockey Employment Training Scheme' - has become a wonderful organisation, helping many jockeys find a new career when their riding days are over. JETS also provides retraining and job search assistance for jockeys who are still riding. The Injured Jockeys' Fund have input and, to keep the competitiveness at a level that jockeys often miss when they are carving out a niche for themselves, there is 'The Griffins Richard Davis Award.' Sadly Richard died after a fall at Southwell racecourse in 1996. All candidates, who have retired from race riding, jockeys still riding and Injured Jockeys' Fund beneficiaries, are eligible to apply for this award.

The rapport and affinity that I have shared over the years with the now 21-year-old horse 'Fiefdom' has given me tremendous pleasure. From the very first day he arrived at Becklyn and I went in the stable with him, he knew I was different. The only way I could feed him mints was by putting one in my mouth and he quickly learnt to take them. He was so gentle right from the beginning. Sean Woods, a friend and now successful trainer, used him for a number of years as a hack to lead his horses. I would go to see him and he always went straight to my face for his treats.

Andy used him for many riding lessons, which he seemed to enjoy, and when my paddock was in need of a good rest Kristien, who was looking after him for me, had the offer of a good paddock in Exning. I wouldn't be able to see him through the office window but my main concern was his welfare now he was in full retirement and 'Fiefdom' deserved the best of everything. He's in good hands. Over the last two years I have not seen him as often as I would have liked, mostly because of my enforced bed rest. Whenever I did go he would put his head through the car window to retrieve a supply of mints! I went to see him a couple of weeks ago and he didn't let me down - as gentle as ever, he only nuzzled and licked my hands when the mints had gone but gnawed dissatisfied at Janet's and Kristien's.

In the mid 80s when 'Pagan Sun' was leaving to be trained in America, I swore I'd never let myself become attached to another Thoroughbred (the dream being fired up all those years ago as a child), but I did - there was always one who I felt needed me. When 'Fiefdom' goes to the stable in the sky it will be the end of my affinity with a racing Thoroughbred, but they will be forever encased in my memory and I will always admire them from afar.

Racing takes many prisoners in different ways: there are lots of stable lads and girls who, even though very capable, never get the chance to pull on the colours and make the majestic walk into the paddock for a ride in a race. Some get that chance but never feel the euphoria of riding a winner. Then there are the jobbing jockeys who manage to make ends meet - just - and the top jockeys, whose life of glamour often comes with the hefty price of wasting their normal weight away. Starving and saunas becomes part of the job - the will to win drives them on and there is no time for anything else. Tunnel vision is required if you want to stay at the top where the competition is fierce but the sportsmanship second to none.

Then of course there are us - victims of the sport we love so dearly. No, we are not victims, we are the unlucky-lucky ones and if I had the chance?

Yes, I'd do it all again.

Because not to have made the journey and found my vocation; to have missed the love of my mother and family or the heart and soul of being in love; to have missed all the hilarious magic moments - the passionate, heart-breaking sad ones that have made up the rich tapestry of my life; to have missed all of this - would be beyond my comprehension.

Not to make each wheelchair-bound day count - now that, too, would be tragic… Truth.

On the Other Side of the Fence

You ask me where I am - I'm here
On the other side of the fence - now
I'm always here - living!
There is no fear.
I can dream of yesterday
No hesitating,
Holding on tightly with one strong finger
Missing all of you - missing the life...
Vividly remembering the thrill of the race
The colours wrapped up in the camaraderie
Of another's plight.
That was my gallop that ended
In a chilling sight,
But in slumber I will not linger.
Salvaging as much as I can
Whilst still making the journey.
I can be the thinker sitting alone
Or join you on the party show.
And hope?
I had the biggest hope of all the hope
Of anyone who passed me by
I cradled it in my arms - yet still it died.
I think I suffocated it with greed
Or with ambition so high,
My home was in the clouds
As I changed - and grew so loud
Shouting from the very top of all the tops
On the land and in the sea.
Letting go of the hand
That once held me.
You cannot make the journey
It's way too far
And I have found a lucky star.

I will always cherish my memory of dreams,
But now - I'm so very pleased
Because this life is just for me.
After all those times
When I was rugged and naïve - it was heaven.
Like life - that sometimes doesn't make sense
But I know I can survive
On the other side of the fence.

Acknowledgements

My thanks to:

Peter Rossdale; one very brave man who let me write this book completely alone - without any regular up-dates after reading the first three scrappy chapters. Mention Sharron and book in the same sentence and Peter - you make me feel as if I can achieve the impossible.

Ian McIntyre; do you really need to put up with my 'whys' and stubborn ways of how I portray certain stories that need some editing - when they seem perfectly clear to me? I think not - but you do, and keep me politically correct as well!

Ian Wallace; from whom I have sought guidance in the past on many queries, but this time I needed to look to myself for the answers - I know you understand and I know who you are now!

Jim McGrath; book launch sorted before the book is written? Now that in the publishing business is a first! I thought that in your line of work you could see when the odds are stacked against you. Not only did this filly have a bad draw but she is also scratchy at the typewriting!

My Ladies; you all assist me to resume normality and appreciate life.

All the girls at EVJ; sorry for the extra work I have put upon you and thank you for putting up with me!